COME INTO HIS PRESENCE

Come Into His Presence

JOHN WALLIS

OVERSEAS MISSIONARY FELLOWSHIP

KINGSWAY PUBLICATIONS
EASTBOURNE

ISBN 0 86065 435 4

Front cover photo: Tony Stone Photolibrary—London

Printed in Great Britain for
KINGSWAY PUBLICATIONS LTD
Lottbridge Drove, Eastbourne, E. Sussex BN23 6NT by
Cox & Wyman Ltd, Reading.
Typeset by CST, Eastbourne, E. Sussex

Contents

Acknowledgements

Thanks for this book must go to numerous friends in the ranks of Overseas Missionary Fellowship and the wide circle associated with that organization. They have taught me so much about prayer, both by their prayers and their dedication to a life keeping in touch with God. They have taken me into the presence of God in such a way as to make me want to do the same for others.

The book would not have been written without the helpful comments of my wife, who also writes for praying people by composing a prayer calendar as part of the bi-monthly OMF magazine *East Asia Millions,* to aid prayer for God's work overseas.

I wish also to acknowledge the untiring contribution of Margaret Gough, my secretary, who typed the manuscript and gave thought to the chapter divisions.

Introduction

It had been a hot sticky day. Soon the drone of the busy traffic would cease as the curfew began. We had been enjoying the cool of the evening sitting in our pocket-handkerchief sized garden. The children were in bed and another day of struggle with Korean language was over.

Before heading off to bed we had turned to prayer in the garden. I forget how long it was that we prayed for, but before we turned in, I said to Kathleen, 'Did you notice anything special about our time of prayer in the garden?' 'Yes,' she said, 'at the end, as we sat there, it was as if the Lord's presence filled the place.' We had, in fact, ceased to verbalize our prayers and had continued to sit in the garden for what seemed like an eternity. I don't think either of us were aware of just how long it was. There was a quite wonderful sense of quiet and stillness. We had drawn near to God in prayer and he had certainly drawn near to us.

I don't think this event would have stayed in my mind so vividly had it not been for an experience some years later when we were back in Scotland, busily engaged in a travelling ministry. I had preached at one of the churches in Ness on the Isle of Lewis. 'The Lord was with you mightily tonight,' said the minister. I had to admit that I felt rather pleased—there is something in all of us that likes affirmation. We went on to discuss what we understood about God's presence with his people, and the minister told me that he had felt one night that his preaching was particularly powerful. Later, however, he and his wife had a time of prayer after supper, and they suddenly sensed that the Lord was present with them. 'We just had to sit still in his presence,' he said. 'There was a remarkable stillness. I would not have thought it special, had not one of my elders called me the next day.' A similar experience was shared, and this was followed by another call from another elder speaking of the same thing. The Lord had clearly drawn near. 'The Lord is in his holy temple; let all the earth keep silence before him' (Habakkuk 2:20). We agreed that believers are the stones of God's temple today and when he comes among his people, they only wish to be still before him. It usually takes a while to know what to say. The sense of his holy presence makes us feel very insignificant. 'Who am I that I should speak to God and live?'

The Bible gives us a most wonderful promise when it says: 'Draw near to God and he will draw near to you' (James 4:8). We believe, because we trust the promises of God, that every time we draw near to God in prayer he does draw near to us—even if we do not always feel his presence. But the Christian life at the end of the day is experiential. The Holy Spirit witnesses with our spirit that we are the children of God, and an experience of his presence is essential if we are to keep going through those times when it seems 'as if the heavens are as brass'.

My experience in that garden in Korea, echoed by the story in Lewis, has left an indelible mark on my life. Of course it is not my only experience of God, but it is a very precious one in my relationship with him. It has brought the conviction that prayer is above all a meeting with God. Through prayer we go into his presence. I find that people who have had some such experience are both more persistent in prayer and more thirsty for the living God. Without any such reality, it is difficult to be an enthusiast for prayer.

Prayer is our greatest need in the church today. All would agree with that. For a variety of reasons, however, we have lost the joy and reality of prayer. I want to write in a practical way so that steps can be taken to recover something that has been lost. This book, therefore, is not so much about our relationship with God, but knowing intimacy with him. The key to being an encourager of others in prayer is to have a real encounter oneself with the living God. And it is God himself who encourages us to meet with him.

So perhaps that ought to be our starting point, for without that we will never enthuse others. Of course, deep experiences of God can not be produced at the touch of a switch, but they can, however, be sought. God in his love promises to meet the deepest desires of our hearts. This is nothing to do with the reasons for Christian assurance—they are more sure and unchanging. But it is everything to do with a Christian's godliness and maturity. There are many experiences abroad in the Christian church today, but it is sobering that in spite of them all the desire for prayer is often lacking.

The comment about the apostle Paul's conversion was surely eloquent here: 'Look, he is praying.' We all know what that was meant to convey. He had found reality as well as forgiveness. He had met the living God and discovered that communion is all to do with God and nothing to do with an empty ceremonial. This is the source of strength that has been the common denominator of God's people down the ages. No wonder

Chinese pastors, imprisoned for twenty years or more, identify so readily with the words of the apostle Paul in prison: 'But the Lord stood by me and gave me strength' (2 Timothy 4:17). They had no alternative but to pray.

I

Whetting the Appetite

A group of Christian leaders were sitting around discussing the proposed half night of prayer at a Student Missionary Conference. Various views were being exchanged. 'There is no virtue in going on into the middle of the night just for the sake of an extended time of prayer,' I said. This was greeted by my Indian and African brothers with astonishment. The brother from India commented that they had a half night of prayer once a month to which whole families came, including children. It was clearly no hardship for them to go through to the early hours in prayer. If the children became tired, they simply took a nap! 'I don't feel the problem will be that the meeting won't go on until the proposed stopping point, but rather that we'll not be able to end it,' said my African friend. I personally had some doubts.

In the event, they were right. As we prayed for God's work around the world, the hours slipped by and it was a discipline to draw the prayer meeting to a close at one o'clock in the morning—in spite of the fact that for some of the students the logistics on campus had not been too good and many of them had had little sleep. I share this to illustrate the point that when God's people make a determined effort to meet with him, he meets with them. At such times, God not only makes his presence felt, but also refreshes his people. The whole experience can be deeply satisfying.

So often prayer is presented as a duty, something that Christian people are expected to do. While we have a clear responsibility to pray, I am convinced that the way to bring about a revival of prayer is not to issue further commands, but to whet the appetite for a deeper experience of God. Was it not something of this nature that prompted the disciples to say to Jesus, 'Lord, teach us to pray'?

It is a strange thing, but western Christians today give less and less attention to prayer. There are a number of reasons for this, particularly our confidence in doing God's work without prayer, because we have so many resources, such as organizational ability, efficient administration and financial power. Also, the more cerebral approach to the Christian faith, and cultural caution over emotionalism in our western spirituality makes us suspicious of depth in prayer. But until we remember again that 'God has made us for himself and our hearts are restless until they find their rest in him', as Augustine put it, we are not likely to seek fresh intimacy with God.

We need to be reminded too that Jesus prayed, in John chapter 17, that his disciples might be where he is, namely in his Father's presence, presumably to enjoy the presence of God. We must not miss this point. The enjoyment of the presence of God is one of the main objectives of the Christian faith. If then time spent in prayer is a wearisome business, something is sadly missing. King David said, 'In thy presence there is fullness of joy' (Psalm 16:11). If we have never tasted something of that joy, then we will not have that desire for his presence.

The strength that comes from enjoying the presence of God in our daily lives will be in short supply.

I want to anticipate some of my readers. I am as aware as anyone of the importance of the balance between biblical knowledge and Christian experience. The important theological questions are where, as believers, we look for Christian experience and what such experience leads us to do. The New Testament direction is to look to Christ for true Christian experience and not elsewhere. There have been many emphases down the centuries purporting to be new, which in fact are as old as New Testament days. They carry us away from Christ and our concentration on him, just as many of the early false emphases did with which the apostle Paul grappled. They make promises which they are not able to fulfil and are in danger of leaving believers with a good measure of spiritual disillusionment. Since all experiences of God's presence in our lives are ministered to us by the Holy Spirit, many such emphases major on the Spirit. Now it is clear that the principal role of the Spirit of God is to make Christ's, and therefore God's, presence a reality in our lives. Both the gifts and the fruit of the Holy Spirit are given to bring near to us the experiential knowledge of the person and character of the Lord Jesus. We need, therefore, to concentrate our thoughts and attention on Christ and his teaching. We will not go astray if we do so. Our spiritual experience will be rooted in the word of God, which makes it clear that it is Christ who both reveals God to us and takes us into his holy presence.

It was Jesus who introduced what was in his day the revolutionary concept of God as a heavenly Father. He taught believers to call God 'Father' and thereby instilled in his disciples a corresponding sense of security in God for all material and spiritual needs, as well as physical protection until we go to heaven, the Father's house and our eternal home. That is the background to so many of the promises that Jesus made concerning answered prayer which major on our relationship with God. As the children of God, we are taught to have confidence in him and draw a genuine security from the relationship.

Here of course is one of the many reasons for a Christian's responsibility to draw others into the same relationship. Jesus commanded us to 'make disciples of all nations, baptizing them in the name of the Father and of the Son and of the Holy Spirit' (Matthew 28:19). The Christian life is a matter primarily of a relationship with the triune personal God. Without such a relationship there cannot be any true enjoyment in life or genuine security.

As the Westminster Confession puts it, 'The first duty of man is to glorify God and to enjoy Him for ever.' Prayer, as much as obedience, must have a central part in that enjoyment. Many of the enjoyments of the Christian life arise from answers to prayer, so if we never actually get down to the matter of praying, we rob ourselves of much that God intends us to enjoy. We neither enjoy him in the place of prayer, nor appreciate him in his response to our prayers. Prayerless Christianity can only lead to joyless Christianity. In seeking a recovery of the prayer life of the church we must learn once again to enjoy God's presence. The experiential knowledge that God loves us is a main spring for believing prayer. Assured of his love, we come to prayer confident that God will hear us and will not fail to answer.

Such assurance is one of the great comforts of the Christian life. It was for this that Christ came into the world, died and opened for us the 'new and living way' into God's presence. It was in this context that the writer to the Hebrews reminded Christians not to give up the habit of meeting together as some were doing. Rather, we are to encourage one another to meet, since the day of the Lord is coming nearer. If that day means anything, it means coming finally and fully into God's presence. It will be the day that will satisfy our total aspirations. Those who are enjoying his presence now look forward to it with anticipation.

The lack of attention today to the Second Coming of Christ is not unrelated. If prayer is both meaningful and satisfying, we will encourage others to pray with us, and look forward to Christ's return to earth. The fact that we do not invite people to times of corporate prayer tells us something is missing in the present enjoyment of God in the life of the church. We have little difficulty inviting others to something we enjoy. Have we lost the necessary incentive to pray? We are hardly going to invite people to an occasion we don't enjoy. The sad fact is that we don't enjoy prayer and the church is in danger of losing its prayer life. We need to have our appetites whetted again for that experience of the presence of God when his people come together to pray.

Prayer

O Lord our God, we confess that we have been content with too little fellowship with you. We rush into your presence, then leave again in a hurry. Whet our appetites for more of your presence. Come among us so that we can say: 'The Lord is in his holy temple, let all the earth keep silent.' May we never leave your presence until we have seen your face and know something of the joy of an encounter with you, the living God. We ask this for your glory and our blessing, in the name of Jesus. Amen.

2

Meetings for Prayer

I meet many Christians today who are sad that the prayer meeting has all but disappeared from the life of their local church. There appears to be a weariness about the coming together of Christians. King David once said, 'I was glad when they said to me, "Let us go to the house of the Lord" ' (Psalm 122:1), but today many Christians seem to lack that sense of anticipation about worship. And it is in worship that the recovery of prayer can begin. If Sunday worship is so unsatisfying, it is bound to be a hard struggle to get Christians to come out to pray together during the week. And if prayer is fundamental to Christian work, which it is, this is a serious gap. I am sure that if Christians learnt to work more by prayer, there would be greater effectiveness and much less frustration, particularly in evangelism.

The Old Testament frequently talks about seeking God. That means a conscious effort to seek the presence of God, through prayer. 'To seek his face' would be another way of putting it. If this is important for prayer, it is likewise for worship. So often worship does not contain a sense of coming into the presence of the Lord with gladness, but rather an atmosphere of a duty being discharged. This is not God's intention. Christ's death on the cross was deliberately designed to usher us into the presence of God following repentance of sin and forgiveness from God. This is the good news of the New Testament. The cross enables us to enjoy an experiential relationship with God which is so joyful, that whenever we come together there is always something for which we can thank God and praise his name. If there is nothing else to praise him for, there is the fact that we know the one and only true and living God, and he knows us.

Part of the responsibility for the lack of prayer in the church must be laid at the feet of pastors and Christian leaders. Very little leadership is given in the matter of prayer today. If the pastor is not enthusiastic about meeting to pray, how can his people be expected to be so? Is this a commentary on the lack of satisfaction many pastors and Christian leaders have in their relationship with God? If for them it is a joyful thing to meet with the Lord, then there will surely be more encouragement given to congregations to meet for prayer.

It would be wrong to conclude from what I have said, however, that when God's people gather together, prayer is always both easy and joyful. Many times it is that way, but there are those occasions when prayer is a battle. Jowett once said, 'There never was a pure season of prayer without a struggle on the threshold.' Those more difficult times of prayer sometimes bring a deeper sense of meeting with God. But since an increasing number of Christian leaders set so little store by prayer, the question arises whether some have missed out themselves in this area of spiritual life. Are there some of us around who need Jacob's ambition? Jacob was the one who wrestled with God until he was blessed. He went away from the presence of God having had his pride broken and for ever aware of his dependence on God.

What a blessing it would be if more of us were dealt with by God in the same way. We need to learn like Jacob that it is only when we are dependent on God that we are blessed and used in Christian service. Can it be that we have lost our sense of dependence on God or indeed ambition for significant experiences of God's presence? Have we lost our appetite to know God, not only in our minds, but in our spiritual experience? Do we no longer wish to be 'dealt with by God' as we say? If this is true for those of us who are Christian leaders, what hope is there for the people of God?

Some fresh leadership is urgently needed for God's people. We need to be able to say confidently that to gather together for prayer can be the most life-changing experience of all, and truly believe it. Andrew Bonar was in no doubt about this for the individual:

> In order to grow in grace, we must be much alone. It is not in society that the soul grows most vigorously. In one single quiet hour of prayer it will often make more progress than in days of company with others. It is in the desert that the dew falls freshest and the air is purest.

The same goes for congregations, but when do they actually get a 'single quiet hour of prayer'?

All major revivals have started with prayer. A significant meeting with the Lord has often restored Christians to the reality of knowing God. There is, of course, more to be said when we are talking about revival, such as the mysterious 'givenness' of prayer. Some Christians talk about a 'burden for revival' or 'a great hunger for God'. God, in his sovereignty, gives this from time to time; it cannot be manufactured. However, revival can be prayed for and sought. Those who experience this 'burden' or 'givenness' in prayer are never the same people again. When revival passes, they hanker after that sense of the presence of God. Like David in the Psalms, they talk of being 'thirsty for the living God'. A visit to the Western Isles of Scotland bears this out, where the effects of the Hebridean Revival in the 1950s remain to this day. Those who remember the revival look for the presence of God in worship, and long for the movement of the Holy Spirit. They approach the prayer meeting with exactly the same attitude.

Is our lack of motivation on the other hand a lack of answered prayer? There is nothing like a clear answer to prayer to encourage us more in our praying. What can renew our relationship with God more? We discover again he is the living God. With King David we say, 'I love the Lord, for he heard my voice; he heard my cry for mercy. Because he turned his ear to me, I will call on him as long as I live' (Psalm 116:1–2, NIV). Part of our trouble is that we have got used to bringing a 'shopping list' to God, without first seeking his face and expressing our dependence on him for the knowledge of his will and the leading of the Holy Spirit, and our prayers are not answered. We fail so often to identify what he wants to do in our lives, the local church, or the wider world. Worse than that we fail to allow Christ to be Lord of his church. There is not so much a lack of faith as a lack of contact with the Lord.

Those who walk with God generally have a good idea of what he wants done, and their prayers are accordingly specific and answered. Too many meetings for prayer which have become a duty, a mere matter of presenting God with our list of requests, have killed the spirit of prayer. We are in urgent need of recovery.

For various reasons, the invitation is not given as it once was to join together for prayer. Our experience of God is so small that we don't care to invite others to our prayer times. We faithfully keep going along as a matter of duty. A fellowship or local church, however, cannot survive long if there is not both real contact with God and clear answers to prayer through the prayer meeting. Since prayer is the most intimate side of the Christian life, when this falters everything else likewise lacks the divine touch. What, then, can be more important than Christians rediscovering the presence of God in their corporate prayer times? Only then will there be more enthusiasm for the prayer meeting.

Prayer

You know, O Lord, all things. You know the poor state of our meetings for prayer. We perform our duty, but are strangers to your divine touch. Forgive our failure to praise and worship you for your own sake. Pardon the pride in us that assumes we know what to pray for and denies your lordship over our lives. O God of Jacob give us a fresh ambition to wrestle with you in prayer and not to let go until you bless us, for your glory. Amen.

3
Entering his Presence

For Christians who have read their Bibles and been taught well, there is no ignorance about the way into God's presence. When the veil of the temple was torn from top to bottom as Jesus died on the cross, symbolically God indicated his desire that his people should come into his presence. Many scriptures remind us that the way into the holy presence of God is through the shed blood of Jesus and that this is the new and living way which he has opened up for all believers. Gone is the necessity for sacrifices to make atonement for sin— Christ achieved that on the cross. As God's children we can now come through his grace into his presence. This is the Christian's greatest privilege and one to be used daily. It is summed up so aptly in Ephesians 2:18 (NIV) where we read that Christians are those who worship God in the Spirit through Jesus Christ 'for through him we both have access to the Father by one Spirit'. The 'both' refers to Jew and Gentile, for this is the way into God's presence which is available to people of every nation. The gift of fellowship with God in prayer is one of those wonderful gifts available to everyone. It is through prayer that fellowship among Christians from around the world is most clearly realized and identified. It is a communication that leaps across the language barriers.

This is basic Christian teaching and yet we need to be reminded of the basis for going into God's presence. Here a little bit more needs to be said, for it is entering God's presence which makes our meetings more than human. They have a divine touch. We have primarily come to meet God. There should be a sense of awe and wonder, reverence and fear. But is that the experience we have in prayer? We can be thankful that in recent years those who have emphasized the importance of praise have taught us something fresh about prayer also. For it is as we praise God, exalting his name and lifting him up with our praises, that we sense his presence and draw near to him. If we look at the Psalms, this was characteristic of the worship of David and others who wrote them. They would first focus on God, rehearsing both his character and wonderful acts, and in the process discover his nearness. The combination of a time of praise and prayer is a wonderful one—the former helps the latter and makes prayer both more humble and vital.

Times of prayer, therefore, need to be prepared as much as any other form of Christian ministry. There is the selection of Psalms and songs, as well as passages of Scripture which remind us of what God has done in the past, confirming his ability to help today. For God has not changed. Such preparation of our hearts for prayer and intercession is indispensable. Some of the requests that we have in our minds become irrelevant. Others come within the bounds of possibility once we have lifted up our hearts in praise of God. Until this is done, with a definite desire to seek God's presence, and a belief that there is something special about his drawing near, our meetings are unlikely to be more satisfying. I am not advocating that we spend all our time in praise and give little attention to prayer, but rather that we come better prepared for intercession. What will happen is that while the prayer meeting may go on for longer than before, that sense of weariness will go. God's people will be refreshed by God's presence. There will be a greater confidence that God has heard and will answer. The prayer meeting which currently holds little appeal for young people will begin to attract them too. They will begin to catch something of the significance of intercessory prayer. The Lord will become above all a prayer-answering God. 'The Lord reigns' will be more than a festal shout.

Let us therefore use the great privilege God has given us of entering his presence, and let us do that in a reverent and spiritual manner, meeting together as if we are coming to the living God. This may mean that Christian leaders have to prepare much more carefully, but surely it is worth the extra effort?

Some complain that young people are only interested in Christian entertainment and have no discipline for prayer. That is not my experience of all, although it is alas true of some. But many have had their appetites whetted for the presence of God through praise and can be led on from that to appreciate the joys of intercessory prayer. If intercession is so fundamental to Christian work, we must find a way to encourage people in this ministry. We must do more than teach its importance —we must get Christians interceding for others.

The importance, then, of realizing the presence of God is great. But how do we do it? The Psalms are so useful here. A study of them shows how time and again they major on the character and wonderful works of God in order to encourage prayer and intercession. It is important to look up to God before we look out into the world with its many pressing needs. If we have a poor perception of the greatness of God, this will correspondingly affect our prayer life. How many prayer meetings have you attended where there has been little sense of worship and no attempt to remind those who have come to pray of the greatness of God? The use of Psalms and spiritual songs can help us greatly to draw near to God. This is a definite activity and not one that should be taken for granted. We are by grace given the privilege of coming into God's presence. We don't have to do anything to earn that privilege, and yet at the same time we do need to realize it in a spiritual and living way. Of course it *is* true that even without a living and emotional experience of the greatness of God, we are in his presence. That is our inheritance by grace. But a prayer time based on the relationship that is ours through God's grace, without the dynamics of that relationship, is a long way from the spirituality of the psalmist and many of the prayers in the New Testament.

The psalmist's struggle with a sense of the absence of God's spirit is the exception rather than the norm. There are those times when 'the heavens seem as brass' and there is little awareness of God's presence. At such times we need to hold on to the promises of God, but even then there is a sense of expectancy within those who have had a powerful sense of the nearness of God and are not satisfied with anything less. Because some times of prayer are dry and difficult, let us not give up seeking a real meeting with God in the power of the Holy Spirit.

For those who have never experienced such a dimension in prayer, however, there is need to encourage them to inherit their inheritance in Christ. It is not enough to know that we have access into God's presence through Jesus Christ. We need also to experience what it means in reality to worship God through Christ in the Spirit.

For that, as we have said, is Paul's description of the Christian community. It must mean more than an intellectual grasp of the church's inheritance through the gospel. If it does not, we have a hard time explaining the changing mood of the psalmist and the apparent spiritual elation he received in the course of waiting in God's presence. To suggest that it was the word of God that lifted him up rather than the Spirit of God is an unhelpful and unnecessary distinction. Word and Spirit go together. The word of God can only truly lift us up if the Spirit is working in our lives.

My concern is that too often, in emphasizing the teaching of God's grace, we under-value the experiences of that same grace. It is important, therefore, to respond to God's word, which says, 'Draw near to God, and he will draw near to you' (James 4:8), and realize that this goes beyond *believing* in the presence of God with his people to actually *experiencing* it. It is a definite spiritual activity whereby in our prayer times we draw near to him. God is personal. That is the wonderful thing about our faith. Our relationship with him, therefore, can be deepened both individually and as a body together in the place of prayer.

Prayer

We thank you, O God, for the privilege of prayer. Thank you for opening the way into your presence. Help us to take hold of our inheritance in Christ and to enter your courts with songs of deliverance. Intercession then, O Lord, will not be in vain, but will be our hope in life's struggles and will bring glory to you in both the church and the world, through Jesus Christ our Saviour. Amen.

4

Discovering in His Presence

The promises of Jesus in connection with prayer are wonderfully broad. For example, 'If you ask anything in my name, I will do it' (John 14:14). To ask in the name of Jesus means not only to exercise our privilege of access to God's presence, but also to be praying in accordance with his will and for the glorifying of his name. Jesus added that he would answer prayer in order that the Father might be glorified through the Son. Part of prayer, therefore, is the discovery of God's will, so that not only may his will be done on earth as it is in heaven, but his glory be seen.

If we are reading our Bibles regularly and understand the general will of God to preach the gospel to all nations, there are a host of things about which we can pray, knowing confidently that they are according to his will. It is the specifics, however, that are difficult. It does not necessarily follow that every Christian event is what God wants. We need to be led by him in our Christian work if the lordship of Christ is to mean anything. It is painfully easy to take on good and worthwhile activities which are not part of his plan for our lives.

This is often the struggle for Christian leadership.

There is the desire that the church should move forward, but along which lines? There is enthusiasm for evangelism, but how are we to do it? There is a desire to have missionary involvement, but in which country and among which people? Here is our need for a more specific understanding of God's will. There has been much discussion over this.

I have always been impressed by the advice that we should get our prayers from God. What does that mean? It means that the Holy Spirit can lead us in prayer and make us aware of God's specific will. Such understanding is received by faith and only time will tell whether our perception has been the true one. Being human, we have to say humbly that many times we misconstrue the will of God. But there is here an aspect of the ministry of the Holy Spirit that helps us in our weakness.

I once heard Dr Martyn Lloyd-Jones suggest that the well-known passage Romans 8:26–27 is speaking to this situation. It is common experience that 'we do not know how to pray as we ought', and often we do not rely upon the Spirit to teach us. Paul goes on, however, to say that the Spirit himself intercedes for us with groans that words cannot express. This seems to suggest that we can receive an understanding of God's will which is difficult to express. This may well be the verse from which we have gained the popular idea of a 'burden' in prayer. It is difficult to describe, but those who have received it know what is meant.

Dr Martyn Lloyd-Jones went on to make the point that the verse, 'He who searches the hearts of men knows what is the mind of the Spirit,' might well refer to those in the prayer meeting who recognize this burden and detect in it that 'givenness' of prayer, or knowledge of the will of God. I am sure that this is a real experience, even if the text means something else! For it seems more likely that it is God who searches our hearts and he knows what he is doing through us by giving such a burden for prayer. As the passage concludes, that burden is the Spirit interceding through us 'according to his purpose'. This is a wonderful encouragement as we think through the crucial matter of praying according to God's will, and therefore being in a position to claim the promises of God associated with prayer.

More recent experiences, as a result of the renewal movement, can help us here too. Paul's emphasis in writing to the Christians in Corinth is that they should be men in their understanding. He is making a plea for maturity. He is putting the emphasis on teaching and knowing the will of God. If we keep that balance, then the interpretation of the gift of tongues, together with prophecy and the word of knowledge or wisdom, can assist us in knowing the will of God in relationship to our intercessions. This moves the purpose of the gifts of the Spirit from experience to understanding. Paul often prayed, as he did for the Colossian Christians, that Christians would grow in their spiritual wisdom and understanding. The gifts of the Spirit can help us do that as God reveals his will and shows us what he would have done. It is surely unbiblical to look upon the gifts of the Spirit as providing us with fresh revelation in terms of Christian truth beyond the Scriptures. On the other hand, it is clear that we need a revelation from God concerning his will. It is often in this situation that the gifts of the Spirit are both helpful and practical. Attention here would, I believe, deliver us from much frustration in Christian work. We need to wait until we believe we know God's will and then work by prayer for its accomplishment.

I remember a missionary sharing with me how, during his time at a Bible school in North Thailand, a student requested permission to go to the shopping centre in town for one or two things. My friend received a word of knowledge that the student's true intention was to go to the bus terminal to meet a girlfriend with whom he was living immorally. Acting in faith and trusting this word of knowledge, my friend announced the student's real intention to him. The man was completely devastated and, in the mercy of God, repented right there on the spot. From that point he never looked back in his Christian life and went on to become a spiritual leader. I cannot say that I have ever had such an experience, but wish to make the point that it is possible to receive precise knowledge from God which forms the basis for faith and action.

We need to recognize this help of the Holy Spirit in our prayer times together. We talk about 'promptings of the Holy Spirit' and should be more trusting of them. As we pray, if God brings particular things to our memory, or seems to lead us forward from what has been previously prayed by another brother, we ought to follow the leading of the Spirit. In this way, we will have growing confidence that we are in God's presence and praying according to his will. By our intercessions we are doing the work of God. I do not believe that anything happens in God's kingdom apart from prayer and when there has been a certain 'givenness' about the prayer time there is a confident expectation of answered prayer and a looking for the way in which the Lord is going to answer. This is part of the enjoyment of the ministry of intercession.

Sometimes we come with very fixed ideas about the will of God, but when we get down to the business of praying, it is not an uncommon experience for the Spirit to work in our hearts and change the direction of our prayers. This can be part of the sanctifying work of the Spirit. Sometimes we realize that our requests are selfish. At other times, we realize that what we are asking for is not for the glory of God, but rather for the glory of our church or institutions. If we do not give ourselves to the activity of prayer, we miss out on this sanctifying work of the Holy Spirit. To put it simply, the Lord deals with us in our praying, showing us that many things on our 'shopping list' are selfish and not needed at all. There is something highly significant about such an encounter through prayer with the living God. It has a cleansing effect.

I believe you can see this in the lives of those who spend a great amount of time in prayer. There is a serenity and composure about such people. Many unnecessary distractions have been removed, to allow a singleness of heart to grow. This level of devotion has been more characteristic of the catholic than the evangelical tradition. There are things that the latter can learn from the former. It is surely subjective, but is there not something about the atmosphere of churches and houses that have been used down the centuries for intercessory prayer? The constant request that God would hallow his name has given such buildings a hallowed feeling. We should be glad that it is still the case that most who seek the refuge of a church building recognize in some way they have come to get right with God. (It does not mean, of course, that God can only be met in specially set-aside buildings, for the joy of the Christian life is that we can meet God in prayer anywhere and at any time.)

In these days of excessive busyness, growing emotional instability and mental breakdowns, even among Christians, we do well to pay more attention to prayer. We live in a very noisy world. The convenience of modern travel has increased the decibels of our world. It is hard to find real quietness. It is, however, very important for Christians to experience the silence of eternity from time to time. Scripture encourages us to be still in God's presence, not only for the healing value of such quietness in our busy, noisy world, but also that we might appreciate the Lord for who he is: 'Be still and know that I am God' (Psalm 46:10).

Initially we are speechless. But to be speechless is not to be Spirit-less. Sitting in the silence of God's presence is to get the right perspective for prayer. This is not a call for empty meditation—which can be deceptively dangerous—but Christians, with the knowledge they have of the word of God, should be able to meditate quietly in the Lord's presence, opening their hearts and lives to the influence of the Holy Spirit so that they might be more aware of the will of God for their lives.

When we talk about the activity of the Holy Spirit in our prayer times, a problem quickly rises concerning those occasions when we have no sense of the Spirit moving among us. The problem of emptiness in prayer. Everything seems lifeless. What do we do at such times? Do we simply give up and go home? I am sure we should respond in the same way as we would when we lack assurance of salvation. We do not rely upon our feelings, but take hold of our faith. We remind ourselves that God has given us access into his presence through the cross, and that the way to God has been opened. Perhaps we can close our eyes and imagine the veil in the temple being torn supernaturally from top to bottom as Jesus died on the cross. It might help to imagine the events surrounding the cross which so dramatically spoke of the new way opened for us into God's presence. When God seems to be absent and inactive, the Bible's answer is to recall those times when we clearly felt him to be both present and active. In a word, we are encouraged to remember God's great acts in history. We can do the same with our own personal history. As John Newton put it:

> His love in time past forbids me to think,
> He'll leave me at last in trouble to sink.

The emptiness of some prayer times may be due to the spiritual struggle in which we are engaged. I am sure that our enemy the devil can throw a wet blanket over prayer times or pour a bucket of cold water on them to persuade us to give up. Satan knows that his kingdom is in danger when God's people pray. Obviously we must not succumb to such enemy interferences. Like tuning in to a radio station, we should keep moving our spiritual dials around until we get through to the presence of God. Sadly, what often happens is that we give up too soon and are not prepared to spend the time required. There is no simple answer to this problem, save that of perseverance. Just as the Scriptures encourage us in the midst of a fresh battle to look back to former victories, so we should look back to other times of Spirit-led prayer to help us get through the difficult empty ones. We need to remind ourselves again and again that the effectiveness of our prayers depends not on the manner or fervour of our praying, but on the merits of Christ's death and heavenly intercession for us. Some of the most difficult times of prayer prove to be the most effective. The important thing is to keep praying. Jesus himself taught his disciples to persevere when he said, 'Men ought always to pray and not lose heart' (Luke 18:1). Just as we are to persevere to obtain our requests, so we should in the first place in order to ascertain God's will in a matter. If we resolve to discover the will of God through prayer we will find it.

Prayer

O Lord, you have said 'seek and you will find'. Help us by your Spirit, to know your will and to persevere until we do. Guide and keep your church in the way of your will that prayer may be more confident and faith rewarded. Thank you that you are more anxious to reveal your will than we are to seek it. May your will be done on earth as it is in heaven, as you direct us by your Spirit. For you have said, 'Whatever you ask in my name, I will do it.' Amen.

5
Preparations

At home when we expect guests, we usually take some trouble to prepare for their coming. This is appreciated by the guests and the preparation helps the whole occasion to go well. In the West we are generally poorer than our Asian friends in this matter, and often don't know how to welcome them. In a well-known hymn we talk about the Holy Spirit being the welcome guest. He certainly is! Why then are the preparations made for times of prayer so often superficial and minimal?

We had a very good time of extended prayer one Saturday evening at our local church. People thanked me afterwards for leading the occasion. While I was grateful to receive their words, I was quick to point out that a great deal of preparation had gone into the event. Ministers and Christian leaders need to prepare as much for the prayer meeting as they do for their sermons. While preparation for the latter is generally understood, often for the former it is not. It may come as a surprise, but it is important to pray for the prayer meeting. If such times are essential to the work of God and the liveliness of our fellowship with him, then prayer is obviously helpful.

We can be very practical about preparations for prayer

times. Having an eye for the layout of the room is valuable, as is creating surroundings which are conducive to worship and prayer. The atmosphere is important. We recognize this for Sunday worship, so why do we fail to see the point for the prayer time? Of course we can pray anywhere and at any time, and the surroundings are not entirely essential. However, they can aid prayer, as can our posture when we pray. In the Bible we read that people stood, sat, knelt and even lay flat on their faces to pray. Sitting with a straight back and in a relaxed position helps us to pray for a long time without discomfort.

It is helpful to have Scripture readings with some explanation of a passage relevant to the occasion. If it is a meeting to pray particularly for God's work overseas, then passages of Scripture speaking of his love for the nations should be used. On the other hand, if it is a meeting to pray for the sick, then the reading of some of the healing miracles of the Lord Jesus in the gospels is helpful. In both cases some short explanation of such passages prepares our hearts for prayer and increases our understanding of the One to whom we will shortly bring our requests.

The same can be said for the choice of music, both hymns and songs, which also should fit in with the theme. Many prayer meetings have been assisted by the use of an overhead projector, noting areas of need for prayer or the names of those for whom prayer is requested. While most of us sit with our eyes closed to pray, it is helpful to have something to look at during the course of an extended time of prayer, reminding us of themes and names. If we are to give ourselves to prayer, then some of these practical matters need to be thought about and appropriate preparations made.

What about nights of prayer? I was impressed by the lead given by the pastor of the Diliman Bible Church in

Manila, Philippines, when announcing the night of prayer. As part of the announcement during the service, he encouraged people to fill in a little response sheet noting items for praise and prayer. These were collected in advance of the meeting, so that they could be put in a proper order ensuring everything would be covered.

His practical exhortation concerning attendance was also helpful. There was no insistence that everyone must stay for the duration of the night of prayer, but it was pointed out that what was not possible on the regular evening for prayer, would be possible in the more extended time. In the context of the Philippines at that time what was meant was the possibility of spending time praying specially for the nation, facing growing restlessness under President Marcos' government and deep concern over the growing strength of the National People's Army in the provinces. There was a real note of urgency about the call to come and pray through the night about the churches' response to the national political situation, as well as their evangelistic outreach.

I am sure that God takes note of nights of prayer and that desire to give undivided attention to the affairs of his kingdom. He honours such times. Not, of course, that we are thinking at all that the longer the time, the more likely God will answer our prayers. Prayer should not be viewed as some eastern-style merit-making ritual. We cannot manipulate God. It is easy to get into this way of thinking, adopting the equation that the longer you pray, the more blessing you will receive. There is blessing in extended times of prayer, because of the time spent in God's presence. It is not, however, automatic. We are talking always about our relationship with God. The motivation for such occasions needs to be clear. It should always be to give undivided attention to seeking God's presence and praying for his glory to be seen in the world. We believe God, in his love, answers prayer, so we want to allow sufficient time to intercede on behalf of his people. We thereby prepare the arena for God to act as he saves, delivers, protects and provides for his people.

When major decisions are being faced, the best preparation is prayer. Jesus himself gave us an example by spending the whole night in prayer before choosing the twelve disciples. How many bad decisions would have been avoided had there been more time spent in prayer? With the increased tempo of life in the twentieth century, such prayer should be more frequent rather than less. We experience more frequent change in society today and the church is no exception. With our increased mobility, there are few congregations that stay the same from one year to the next. There is constant need to appoint leaders, train others, assess people's contribution and review programmes. All this calls for more prayer not less. The absence in many churches of such prayer is a sad loss. Given adequate preparation, such occasions can enrich the life of a local church and be a turning point, not only in the affairs of the church locally, but also further afield in the nation and abroad. If it is God's work we are doing, we would do well to make sure he is the principal guest when we meet to pray, and prepare accordingly.

Prayer

Thank you for the joy of welcoming guests to our homes. Help us, O Lord, to prepare for your coming to our meetings for prayer. Gracious Spirit, Holy Ghost, you are the guest we covet most. Come to us to inform our minds and to inspire our hearts. Lead us to Christ, that he might preside over our meetings. When we call on

him may we also acknowledge his lordship for the sake
of his kingdom. Amen.

6

Promises

The prophet Samuel said once, 'far be it from me that I should sin against the Lord by ceasing to pray for you' (1 Samuel 12:23). The Bible teaches us to pray for the rulers of nations and Samuel was aware of the importance of so doing. By these words he made a covenant to pray for the king, although we are not told how frequently. Samuel, being a priest, would have had regular times for prayer. No doubt he prayed for the king each day. It is surprising how little Christians pray for their national leaders and governments. We believe that the Lord is the ruler of all nations, and yet do not act accordingly. Such was Samuel's concern for the nation that he made a covenant to pray for the king.

What place should such covenants have in the life of a Christian? In the emotion of a meeting it is easy to promise to pray—for example, for those leaving for the mission field—but we often fail to fulfil our promise. There is value, however, in making a covenant to pray for others and taking steps to fulfil that covenant. Many of us find it difficult to be disciplined about prayer. The act of making a covenant can help us. Of course we shall fail, being weak and human, but a promise can help us to be more faithful and remind us of the good intentions we had once, when we made our promise.

It is not fashionable these days to think of regular times for prayer. We don't like to bring together discipline and devotion. If we are honest, however, we have to admit that we need the discipline of setting aside regular times for prayer. It appears that Daniel prayed three times a day, facing Jerusalem the Holy City each time. We know that Muslims pray five times a day, being reminded to do so by the call to prayer from the mosque. While we have no desire to be religious about prayer, we certainly ought to take steps to pray regularly. This is something that individuals like churches have to decide for themselves. Once a discipline has been agreed, however, we do well to try to keep it.

In Korea and other parts of Asia today, the idea of a dawn prayer meeting has been one accepted pattern of discipline for some years now. In days during missionary service in Korea, it was not easy to get up in the early hours to attend the dawn prayer service. I had questions, like other missionaries, about the value of such meetings. However, there were occasions when the weariness of the flesh was transformed by deep fellowship with God in prayer. The discipline ensured that one had met with the Lord before meeting with other people. The idea of an early morning quiet time has been essential for some evangelical Christians for many years. The main point of such times is that we have an opportunity to hear from God through his word and to lay the needs of the day before him in prayer, before getting involved with others. It should not be looked upon as a rule that cannot be broken, but rather a discipline that is helpful. If we lack discipline then all too easily other things swallow up those vital times of prayer.

In the ministry of Jesus and the early church, special

times were set aside for prayer and fasting. Generally speaking, these were when important decisions were being faced, or particular opposition was coming to the message of the gospel. The need for such days of prayer for the local church and indeed Christian work generally cannot be over-stressed. It gives clear expression to our conviction that Jesus is Lord of the church and we are under his headship. Family problems, both within and without the church, have been solved through days of prayer. If we would learn to talk more to God and less among ourselves, we would rejoice in the wonderful working of the Holy Spirit resolving problems and uniting God's people. God does speak to his people, both individually and collectively, when they take the trouble to meet for prayer.

For most Christians there is the regular covenant to meet with God for worship on the Lord's day, Sunday. (There are some few Christians, of course, who do not note Sunday as special beyond other days.) Generally speaking, where there is freedom to worship the Lord and keep Sunday special for that, the discipline of Sunday worship is one way of making a covenant with God to pray. How inflexible we Christians are in the use of Sunday! God has given us this one day for rest and worship, and yet we manage either to make it such a busy day that we are not refreshed for the responsibilities of the rest of the week, or so minimal in its programme as to be of little use in developing our spiritual lives. In the pressure to find a suitable time to meet together to pray, I wonder why more consideration of the use of Sunday is not given.

Some fellowships today have begun to see the value of using Sunday more creatively. Instead of sticking to the pattern of morning and evening services, some gather in the morning for an extended time of worship, then have a fellowship meal together using the early part of the afternoon for prayer and committee work. Following that, the rest of the day is used for leisure and recreation with the family. If we view Sundays as those special days for developing our love relationship with the Lord, we will make them as creative as possible. In a marriage relationship there needs to be those times when husband and wife can be together to build their marriage and enjoy one another. Should not the bride of Christ likewise use Sundays for a deepening of her love relationship with the Lord and enjoying his presence?

There are many other ways of making covenants to pray. Small group prayer meetings for special needs have been used greatly over the years to extend God's kingdom. Those with a common desire can meet together to pray—perhaps for missionary work, or evangelistic outreach, or the social work of the church. Generally such groups can be more accurately informed of situations and are able to pray through every aspect of the work. There are also those whom we might call 'prayer partners' who undertake to pray for Christian workers and missionaries (their 'partners' in prayer) on a regular basis. It is encouraging to see how many are able to make this kind of covenant to pray. Such is their involvement that the promise to pray daily is no hardship. They usually do this during their personal daily time of quiet, receiving regular information to help their praying. A deep empathy with those for whom they pray develops, and their intercessions are as important as the actual work being done. Some I know keep a diary noting what is prayed for each day and recording answers to prayer. People who have prayed in this way for many years can testify to the fact that most of their requests have been answered. You would have a hard job persuading such people that prayer is ineffective. When on the rare occasion prayer is not answered, a reassessment of those requests can often reveal that a redirection of the work is necessary.

It is hard for us to understand why God has limited his work in the world to the prayers of his people. But generally speaking that is what he has done, and we can count on his help when we make promises to pray and exercise some discipline in the matter, both as a local church and as individuals.

Prayer

Forgive us, O Lord, for all those promises we have made to pray and have failed to keep. Help us to be faithful in keeping all such promises. We acknowledge our need of discipline in prayer, for although the spirit is willing, and the understanding clear, the flesh is weak. Above all help us to keep our covenant to worship you on the Lord's day, and to use your day more creatively for prayer. We ask this for the coming of your glory in all the world. Amen.

7
Disappointments

The church's experience in the matter of prayer is that it is answered regularly and frequently. If the Lord Jesus has promised to answer prayer, which he has, then that is what we should expect. Similarly, for the individual Christian, his life is punctuated with answers to prayer. In this way, both the Christian community and the individual discover more and more of God's love and grace. In daily experience God's love is unfailing.

It is quite different in other religions where there is no assurance of answered prayer. I once asked a taxi driver in Kuala Lumpur what the sign in his taxi written in Arabic meant. 'The Spirit of God will look after you,' he said. He explained that as he was a Muslim and went regularly on Fridays to the mosque, as well as kept the five times of prayer daily, many blessings came his way. 'Have you received many answers to your prayers then?' I asked.

'Oh no,' he said, 'but if you keep the rules of Allah you will get blessing.'

Clearly in Islam, there is no door to a personal relationship with God and no assurance of answered prayer. Life is simply locked up to fate. Everything comes from Allah, good or bad, and there is little that can be done about it. Good works or keeping the rules, however, are meant to ensure blessing or prosperity.

How then do Christians handle the matter of un-answered prayer? This has always tested the faith of God's people down the years. The psalmist often com-plains that while he lives righteously and prays to God, it is the wicked who seem to flourish and the ungodly who go unchecked. Psalm 73 is a good example of this. How-ever, the wisdom gained through entering into God's presence caused the psalmist to realize that the blessings of God are not limited to this life and if certain things are withheld, then there is a good purpose behind it. The knowledge that God loves us is fundamental to coping with unanswered prayer. The Christian knows that God is always working for his good, and unanswered prayer is not to be read as a lack of concern on God's behalf. Rather, such situations are a call for trust and obedience. It has been said that since unanswered prayer is not the norm, such times are full of instruction. We need to look for the lessons of unanswered prayer.

What is God saying when he does not answer prayer? We may be praying for a friend to come to Christ, but it may not be God's time to save him. We may feel we have a particular need, but it may be more a matter of what we want rather than what we need. We may long for revival in a nation, and when the church is so weak and the nation increasingly turning away from him, our cry becomes desperate, but for some reason God does not appear to answer. We come to appreciate that God has a time for revival.

In all these situations we have to trust the sovereign purposes of God without questioning his love. This is even more crucial when it comes to such painful situ-ations as the death of a loved one after prayer has been made for his recovery. At such times our hold on fundamental Christian doctrine is so important. Paul says that to depart and be with Christ is far better, and although we may find that hard to accept, in reality death is not loss for the Christian, but only gain. The perspective of eternity is important. While not minimising the bereavement, we should be sad, but not like those who have no hope beyond the grave. It is often by passing through deep experiences of this order that we discover more of the love of God. We are surprised both at the grace God gives and the love of the church, his people. What seemed an impossibility becomes a possibility in answer to our prayers. The fear of loneliness and inability to cope are removed. While God has not answered prayer in the way we would wish, he has done so in other ways.

While it is true, as the psalmist puts it, 'If I had cherished iniquity in my heart, the Lord would not have listened' (Psalm 66:18), we need to be very careful not to place the blame for unanswered prayer on ourselves. We have a natural disposition towards justification by works and towards feeling that it is because our lives are not good enough for God that our prayers are not being answered. It is true that God will withhold his blessing if we persist in sin, but the problem rarely lies there, but rather in a sense of personal unworthiness for God to hear and answer our prayers. The answer to this is to be reminded that any answer to prayer is due entirely to God's unmerited favour and his unfailing love. We are heard simply because Christ has died for the forgiveness of our sins and made us acceptable to our heavenly Father. It is wrong, therefore, to punish ourselves when prayer is not answered with thoughts of inadequacy or lack of spirituality.

A positive way to face unanswered prayer is to ask further questions. What is God saying in this situation?

He may be putting the finger on some personal or corporate sin. God did not answer Joshua's prayers to take the city of Ai because of Aachan's sin. But more often the Lord is redirecting the prayers of his people. It may seem a good idea to start a fresh outreach into a particular district or overseas, but then we do not know all the circumstances and such an outreach may not be within the present plan of God and will lead only to frustration.

Western society is largely motivated by achievement, so many of us are by disposition ambitious. There is nothing wrong with ambition, provided it is an ambition God has for us. He may, however, curb our ambition in order that we might learn a little bit more about relationships. While it is good in life to have goals, it is also important to achieve them in the right way. We don't believe the end justifies the means and if other people get in the way of our ambitions, then we need to know how to handle that. God may well frustrate us at this very point in order to teach us that relationships are more important than our secret ambitions.

If this is our approach when faced with disappointments in prayer, then we shall not be too discouraged. We will not doubt that God has heard, but understand that for some good reasons, he is withholding the answer. Unanswered prayer will become a school for learning more about God's ways with his people and his sovereign purposes.

We should not forget either that 'no' is an answer to prayer. In retrospect we can often see how kind God has been in not giving us all we have wanted. Jesus in commenting that human fathers know how to give good gifts to their children states that God as our Father will always give good gifts to his children, especially the gift of the Holy Spirit. His answer may well be the power of the Holy Spirit to cope with a difficult or disagreeable situation.

Similarly, the answer 'wait' is as significant as any other answer to prayer. There is a time in God's economy for everything. We do well to be patient for it. The directors of OMF were urgent in their desire to develop the international headquarters in Singapore, but there were many frustrations and delays. Today the building is going ahead at a fraction of the original costs due to an unforeseen slump in the economy in Singapore. In the intervening years God answered prayer by giving his grace to accept the cramped conditions and also by refining the original plans. In retrospect we can thank God that the answer 'wait' was patiently accepted. The end result will be to the glory of God.

Prayer

We thank you, Lord, that your love never changes. Help us not to interpret your failure to answer our prayers as your failure to care for us. Forgive the unbelief that so easily misinterprets your actions. Make us patient in the knowledge that you have something better in store, and when the going is tough help us to discover that underneath are the everlasting arms of your love. We ask this in the name of the One who said, 'If it be possible, let this cup pass from me.' Amen.

8

Helping Others

Larger corporate times of prayer for some people are not easy. Many find it difficult to pray aloud in public. Those who are more used to doing so may unwittingly put beginners off. Some pray at such length that the shorter one sentence prayer seems rather immature by comparison. Then by dint of experience some pray using a great deal of jargon. If you stop to listen to the way people pray, how many phrases are repeated again and again? How often do people 'just' want the Lord to do this and that! Why do we 'just' want this and that, when really we would much prefer he answer our prayers way above our expectations? Paul said that this is precisely what he does do, since he is the One who is 'able to do immeasurably more than all we ask or imagine according to his power that is at work within us' (Ephesians 3:20). We are all creatures of habit and it is hard to get away from jargon and to pray more briefly if we are used to praying at length. Worse, in using special Christian terms, we forget the newcomers who have not heard them before.

When we realize some of the difficulties of corporate prayer, we can see the wisdom in using some of the time to divide into twos and threes. People find it easier to pray in a cell rather than in a body. One of the hindrances to praying with others is that we don't really know people. If we knew one another better we would feel less shy about articulating our prayers. When we divide into groups it helps us to get to know people more intimately and gives the security some need for opening their mouths in prayer.

While it is quite commonplace in other parts of the world, particularly in Asia, for all present to pray aloud together so that the volume of prayer sounds like the rushing of mighty waters, such praying is generally less common with groups of western Christians. The Asian method has its value however. Those who have experienced it speak of blessing. It is an opportunity for free expression of one's love for the Lord and to praise him, as well as making a personal response to the ministry of God's word. In Asian churches, very often such times of prayer follow the preaching of the word of God and are intended to be a response to the deeper understanding received about the Lord.

At such times, many who have the gift of tongues use their prayer language. If we are anxious to help others, we need to think carefully about this, because for some this is difficult to accept. If there are those in the group who do not accept that the gift of tongues is relevant today, we present them with an even greater problem. At the end of the day we need to ask what is best from the point of view of the local cultural pattern and the unity of the body of Christ. I have talked to Asian Christians and certainly they do not struggle at all with corporate times of prayer when everyone praises God at the same time. Many of them too are not inhibited when others pray in tongues. In many Asian churches there are people with different languages and members themselves usually speak more than one. For those of us who can only speak English, with little experience of other languages, we can find such times of prayer threatening.

The reason for mentioning these things is that if we want the prayer meeting to grow in depth, then we must take steps to ensure that everyone is able to participate. If the way forward is to pray in groups then let us not stick to the traditional pattern. We can, of course, pray in silence in the quietness of our own hearts, but the Scriptures indicate that the norm is to verbalize our prayers. This can be a significant growth point for Christians, and their experience of God's help in their praying can lead to a deeper experience of the power of the Holy Spirit.

In isolating some of the difficulties in corporate times of prayer, let us not swing to the opposite extreme by concluding that it would be better if we stuck to liturgical prayers, as helpful as they are, or private prayers at home.

The prayer meeting plays an important role in creating a sense of community among God's people. As we praise God for what he has done, and pray for those things we believe to be in his plan, a sense of community develops and we begin to recognize ourselves as the people of God on the march, capturing fresh territory for the kingdom of God under the authority and leadership of the Lord. When the church is persecuted, this sense of community grows. It is not simply that I am being opposed because I am a Christian, but rather that the people of God are under attack because of the activity of the enemy. Like the early church we can pray, 'Consider their threats and enable your servants to speak your word with great boldness' (Acts 4:29, NIV).

The sense of community is important. We need to find a way whereby we can transfer some of the marvellous

Old Testament stories of the victories of Israel through prayer to the ongoing work of the local congregation. Think of the fall of Jericho, which was brought about by reliance on God expressed in worship and praise as the people marched around the city. What about the victory secured in the days of Jehoshaphat written up in 2 Chronicles 20? As the people went out to battle, they did so in an attitude of trust and praise to God for the victory. The battle was won even without the Israelites making physical contact with the enemy, since in the panic the opposition destroyed one another.

How often, after prayer, do we discover that the gathering black clouds of mounting opposition fade away. The Lord has acted for us and given the victory. If the correlation becomes apparent, people's confidence in prayer grows. They begin to sense they are part of the people of God engaging the enemy and gaining the victory. The prayer meeting can no longer be viewed as an adjunct to the church's work. If we are not seeing answers to prayer, it is very easy for the church to be seen as a human organization, and any progress to be related to the hard work of the congregation or the business efficiency of the administration. The success of some churches, of course, does depend on these things, which are necessary. If, however, that is all there is to the life of the church, then we are missing God's intention for his people. A successful church is not necessarily a spiritual church. Some churches would go further with some business efficiency, but no amount of human organization can ever bring true spiritual progress to a local congregation, nor effectively extend God's kingdom. Only prayer can do that.

The other great advantage of living as God's community is that individuals no longer feel alone with their problems and difficulties. It becomes more natural to share these with the congregation and for Christians to grow accustomed to others praying for them. In this way Jesus' command that we should love one another receives practical expression and individuals begin to receive the love of Christ through the body of believers. If I am not particularly feeling the nearness of Christ in my own private devotional life, it is a great encouragement to discover Christ's love through the ministry of the body of the local congregation. For many good reasons, therefore, we should take care to help one another in our corporate times of prayer. Christian leaders need to give every encouragement to believers to unite for prayer. Some leaders reserve their choicest bits of news for the prayer meeting. Others invite those who have been away visiting Christians overseas to report to those who meet to pray. Often they are the ones who have been praying about the journeys. I remember one such occasion when we received news from Eastern Europe, Africa and an inner-city situation in Britain. The encouragement from what God was doing elsewhere provided the motivation to pray he would do similar things in the local community. With a little imagination we can get the prayer meeting back on the agenda of Christians' priorities.

Prayer

Open our lips, Lord, that we might speak your praise and teach us how to pray. Take away our fear of others and remind us that you look on the heart and are more concerned with our thoughts than our powers of expression. May we discover the power of the Holy Spirit as we call on your name and give us the joy of interceding for others. Help us not to hinder others in prayer, but encourage them to make the same discovery too. For Jesus' sake. Amen.

9

Unbroken Communion

A look at the life of Jesus, as given in the gospels, leaves
the distinct impression that he maintained a constant
communion with his Father in heaven. Statements like,
'I only do those things the Father tells me,' speak of a life
guided continually by the Spirit of God, so that no part
of it was wasted. The challenge to Christian living is
clear. By walking in the steps of Jesus we should likewise
enjoy a daily communion with God, so that none of our
time is wasted. Paul exhorts us to redeem the time because the days are evil. It is easy to be distracted by the
enemy of God's work, engage in fruitless activity and
waste precious time. 'Are there not twelve hours in a
day?' said Jesus. He was reminding his disciples that
God gives time for everything he wants us to do. However, without sensitivity to the Holy Spirit, we shall find
that we run out of time for doing God's work according
to his timetable for our lives. There will be some unnecessary regrets.

Down the centuries, many have tried to 'practise the
presence of God' in their daily lives. Classics have been
written on this subject, like the book by Brother Law-
rence. There is an important truth here. In a sense, as

Christians, we cannot survive without prayer. This is driven home in the very chapter in John's gospel which is full of Jesus' command to live in him. Using the illustration of the vine, he reminds us that unless we are attached to him, we will be without effect in the world.

It is all summed up in those startling words, 'Without me, you can do nothing.'

We tend to suppose there are quite a lot of things we can do without the Lord Jesus and that it is only for the big things in life we need his help. This is part of our pride, for we hate to be totally dependent on God, surrounded as we are by the spirit of humanism or self-sufficiency, amply enforced by scientific and technological developments. It is hard for modern man to cultivate a spirit of dependence on God for every aspect of his life. Even although we know that we depend on God for every breath we breathe, we are slower to realize our dependence upon Jesus for holiness of life and effectiveness in Christian work. It is those who have learnt to live by unbroken communion with the Lord who are the most effective in living the Christian life and helping others spiritually. It is right to emphasize daily times of quiet and a disciplined devotional pattern, but we shouldn't leave the presence of God once our devotional time is over. We must learn to walk with God through each day. If we do, missing our quiet time with God will not be accompanied by pangs of smitten conscience. We are talking about a way of life, not a meritorious work to receive some mystical blessing. We will rather regret the lost opportunity to listen to God and talk to him.

This becomes more critical when we think of Christian witness. If we are truly in fellowship with the Lord Jesus and his life is being lived out in ours, there will be plenty of opportunities to give 'a reason for the hope that is within us'. The Bible's expectation is that our lifestyle should cause people to ask questions, so that we can tell them why we live the way we do.

Paul made the point to the Colossians by exhorting them to be always 'gracious, seasoned with salt, so that you may know how you ought to answer everyone' (Colossians 4:6). The implication is that people will enquire about our lifestyle, and the things to which we give our time and attention. If they don't, perhaps we are missing the mark. The way we treat our neighbour will only be right if we are in a right relationship with God. Such treatment should provoke comment! This is both the challenge and the joy of the Christian life. Opportunities for witnessing to Christ should arise naturally as a result of our communion with God.

Christian work is done in the name of Jesus. To serve others in his name is to act under Jesus' authority and in his power. The love we express for our neighbour can be of that order. Jesus has commanded us to love our neighbour without qualification and that is only possible by his grace. We find it much easier to love ourselves first, rather than love our neighbour as ourselves. In facing some of the needs others have, we quickly realize how helpless we are. Often we do not wish to get involved in other people's lives simply because their problems are overwhelming and there appears to be no answer. This surely is to limit the power of Christ and to underestimate the power of prayer.

The apostles coped with such things by ministering to others in the name of Jesus. Acutely aware of their own inability to help, they learnt how to bring the help of Jesus to bear on different situations. The results were quite spectacular. The lame were made to walk, the blind to see, the sick healed and the unrepentant judged. One of the central points of debate in the church today is how far we can expect Jesus to manifest his power and glory as we serve him in the world. Some see no theological justification, or realistic expectation, for similar events to happen today. Others, submitting to the sovereignty of God in his ways with men and women, have a greater expectation in serving others in the name of Jesus and have seen some remarkable things happen.

Some months ago, I sat before a middle-aged woman trying to come to terms with what had happened in her body as a result of prayer and the laying on of hands. A ministry team had come to her home—moved with love for her. For two years she had suffered as a result of the birth of her first child with a wound that required delicate surgery. They had prayed for her just a few days before she saw the gynaecologist who was to perform the operation, and he had discovered on examination that it was no longer needed. The doctors had no explanation, and neither had this missionary mother. She was instead trying to adjust to this dimension in the power of prayer.

Out of the ten lepers healed by the Lord Jesus, only one returned to give thanks and presumably became one of his disciples. We might expect a similar pattern today. Many friends for whom we have prayed, having received God's help and healing, show no further interest when the crisis is over. The central issue will always be repentance and whether or not in response to God's mercy they recognize who Jesus is and begin to obey him. The surrender of lives to the authority and lordship of Jesus Christ will not happen without prayer. God needs to give us grace to repent. Without his working in our hearts there will be no faith and obedience in the Lord Jesus, no matter how many temporal blessings we receive from his hand.

How essential communion with God is for both Christian living and Christian service. One of the greatest encouragements in prayer is to see what is possible in daily life when we pray about the quality of our lives and service to others. Just as prayer grows, so does faith. Jesus promises to answer prayer if there is faith the size of a grain of mustard seed, but he does not intend that our faith remain so small. We are to become more adventurous in prayer and faith, and as we do so our communion with God deepens, and we can begin to say, like Jesus, 'I only do those things the Father tells me.'

Prayer

O Lord, without you we can do nothing. We can neither pray effectively nor serve acceptably. Deliver us from trying to do either in our own strength and help us to rely on you. So deepen our communion with you that your life becomes our life and your works become our works. May our communion with you be more constant that others may recognize we are about your Father's business, and come to know you through the witness of your church. For your glory. Amen.

10

Promptings

The gentle, yet persistent, influence of the Holy Spirit is
something that we recognize more readily during times
of prayer, whether they be personal or corporate. We
often talk about being prompted in our praying by the
Holy Spirit. It is difficult, of course, to articulate exactly
what we mean by that phrase, but it is that sense of being
led by the Holy Spirit to pray for a particular matter or in
a particular direction. Those who spend a great deal of
time in prayer are perhaps more aware of these promptings than others. It has to do with our walk or relationship with God—our ability to sense his presence and be
directed by him, particularly in the discipline of prayer.

Sensitivity to what the Spirit is saying to the churches
is important. Some are more sensitive than others in this
area, but all of us from time to time have a sense of
compulsion to pray about certain individuals or situations. This prompting should not be dismissed lightly,
but responded to. If we believe, as I do, that God limits
his work in the world to the prayers of his people, then
we should be able to understand why this is so important. It is the Spirit who is wanting to work through us,
teaching us to intercede according to the will of God.

Does he find us responsive or somewhat doubting?

To illustrate the importance of responding to the Spirit's promptings here is the true story of two CIM missionaries during their days in China many years ago. They were under house arrest during the occupation of the Japanese prior to World War II and living in quite a substantial house. Many of their Chinese friends came to stay with them for protection, and during those days there were many wonderful answers to prayer. There was a shortage of meat and, in answer to prayer, for three consecutive days the Lord arranged for a beautiful Chinese crane to perch in the tree in the garden. Each time the bird was bagged and put in the pot! Crane is as good as chicken, or so I am told.

There then followed quite an unexpected turn of events when the two missionaries concerned were taken before the Japanese authorities, charged, and condemned to death. Since this was all conducted in Japanese, they were ignorant as to why they were being sentenced so harshly.

They found themselves facing a firing squad in the town square. Certain that their end had come, the older missionary was encouraging his younger colleague to be 'faithful unto death'. The order to load had been given, but then a high-ranking Japanese officer appeared on the square astonished to discover what was going on. He promptly disbanded the firing squad, apologised to the missionaries and ended their house arrest!

It was months later, when reporting this incident and marvellous deliverance at a prayer meeting in Australia, that a woman left the meeting to return to her home to look at her diary. She then returned to speak to one of the other ladies present in the prayer meeting. She reminded her how on that particular day they had met in the street and she had spoken about her concern for the missionaries in question. Together the two ladies had gone to her home and spent considerable time in prayer. On checking the time difference, it was discovered that as the two ladies were praying in Australia, the two missionaries were facing the firing squad in China. What might have been the situation, had that woman not responded to the promptings of the Holy Spirit? We shall never know.

From time to time the veil of mystery concerning prayer is drawn back and the vital relationship revealed. Prayer is not only a matter of responding to such promptings, but this clearly plays an important part. As to why God channels his help through the prayers of his people, I can only make the suggestion that it is in order that such deliverances be seen to be from God alone and the glory, therefore, be given to him. We have already spoken about this activity of the Spirit of God in corporate times of prayer. If we were more responsive, there would surely be a greater sense of being led in prayer and of getting our prayers from God. The coming of God's kingdom, after all, is more a matter of his activity than ours, and some of the effectiveness of prayer is lost when we ignore such promptings.

There is also another kind of prompting that needs to be recognized. When it comes to decision making, Christians also speak about being led by the Lord. It is easier to see how we have been led by the Lord when we look back and clearly see his guidance over a particular decision. When there has been prayer, particularly for guidance in evangelism, the results are often encouraging. In praying for those to whom we wish to pass on the good news, quite often the opportunity to do so comes naturally, yet clearly as a result of prayer.

I heard of a couple involved in street evangelism who spent considerable time in prayer and fasting before undertaking visitation through a district. Rather than go slavishly from door to door, they prayed that God would lead them to those homes where he could use their testimony. As they walked down the roads of the district they were attempting to sensitize themselves to the leading of God's Spirit. At one house they interrupted the patter of a Jehovah's Witness with the words 'Jesus loves you', whereupon he dissolved into tears and immediately asked for spiritual help. At another house the occupant announced that he had been waiting for their visit, believing that God was going to send someone to him that day. No doubt there were other disappointing visits, but there was sufficient encouragement to show that they were being led by God as a result of prayer.

This is nothing new, of course, as we think of Philip the evangelist, who was spoken to so directly by the Holy Spirit and led to the Ethiopian eunuch with marvellous results. The story is found in Acts 8, and while its inclusion is probably intended more to provide us with an illustration to show that the nations were seeking the Messiah right from the beginning, it also teaches very clearly the way in which the evangelist, provided there is prayer, can be led to people in whose hearts God's Spirit is already at work.

If on the one hand obedience to Christ's command to take the good news to all nations is required, on the other hand the discipline of regular prayer coupled with a high expectation of God's leading is also essential. Doubt concerning the effectiveness of such prayer, together with a reluctance to be led by the Spirit of God, robs us of success in evangelism. Similarly, how many of our fellow believers are being left without the protection of God or his loving provision, because we fail to respond in prayer when the Lord brings to us some timely reminder of them? We shall never know this side of heaven, but I suspect we shall be surprised beyond measure at what God has done in response to the prayers of his faithful people.

Prayer

We thank you, O Lord, that you still communicate with your people by the Holy Spirit. Make us sensitive to the leading of the Spirit in prayer. May your word and Spirit be our guide as we serve you in the extension of your kingdom, so that we might be the channels of your blessing to others. May we help others by our prayers as you stir us up to pray, and teach us not to quench the Spirit, who is sent to intercede through us for the needs of others. Amen.

I I

Protections

After my wife and I had spoken at the farewell service arranged for us by our local church, which commissioned us for work in South Korea, no less than three separate individuals came and gave to us Psalm 91 as a word from God for our time abroad. It is a Psalm, full of comfort. We quickly concluded two things. The first was that God would protect us from 'the arrow that flies by day and the disease that stalks by night' and the second that in his mercy he would give to us a long life.

As things worked out we were wonderfully preserved. In the summer in Korea, a particularly vicious kind of scorpion appears. These unfriendly intruders have a dreadful bite which can only be survived by the use of morphine. Never once were we or our children the victims of their vicious attack. Likewise, during the winter, many Korean homes are heated by an ancient but effective heating system, depending for its success on a fire of coal briquettes at one end of the house and underfloor flues drawing off the heat and gases to the other end and out through a long chimney. On one occasion, my son and I were mercifully delivered from carbon monoxide poisoning when we were staying at a friend's house. The guest room floor had not received adequate attention in recent months, and deadly carbon monoxide gas was seeping into the atmosphere. My wife, 400 miles away and pregnant with our third child, was woken up with abdominal pains and filled with concern for her husband and son rather than herself. Her prayers for our well-being and safety led to the waking of my son with similar abdominal pains and our deliverance from almost certain catastrophe. You can imagine the rejoicing when the two sides of the story were eventually put together.

However, in spite of many assurances of God's protection as a result of prayer, things don't always work out the way we think they should. Why was it that when earnest prayer was made on behalf of Peter by the church, he was miraculously released from prison, whereas James was beheaded by Herod? Why was it that prayer was effective in one case, but not in the other? We have to rest here in the essential goodness of the sovereign purposes of God. So often where there is a response of faith in a loving God, tragedy is turned into triumph.

Because we in the West are so unused to suffering for the cause of the gospel, we tend to conclude that imprisonment, or other such trials, is about the worst thing that could happen to us. How much we have to learn from others. Nepali pastors, who are frequently put in prison, ask their friends to pray not that they will be spared imprisonment, but that their sentence may be less than one year. They believe that to be in prison for more than one year is more than their families can bear! Apparently, separation of up to a year is gladly accepted as part of being a Christian leader. I have had the privilege of meeting many pastors in Korea who have suffered in prison for their faith. During the time of the Japanese occupation of the Korean peninsula many pastors refused to bow at the shinto shrine signifying their allegiance to the Emperor of Japan as divine. While undoubtedly the suffering was great, the blessing appeared to be greater. They proved, as Paul put it, that 'all things work together for good to them that love God' (Romans 8:28, Authorized Version). In their case, as in many others, God's protection prevented bitterness and hardness of heart creeping into their lives and spoiling their testimony.

We need to learn that the Lord has a special way for each one of his children. The important thing is that we follow him rather than look at his pathway for others. This was exactly the point the Lord Jesus made with Peter, when he was asked what was going to happen to John. 'What is that to you?' said Jesus. 'Follow me!' (John 21:20–22). When faced with suffering, our response should always be to turn to the Lord in prayer. Many Christians have spoken about the blessing of 'the fellowship of his sufferings' and the remarkable effects of prayer at such times.

One further story illustrates this well. On a visit to Poland, I was introduced to my interpreter who seemed to have a particular charisma and dynamism about him. His interpretation was both good and powerful. I quickly discovered that he was a man of prayer. He was convinced of the value of prayer through his own experience. Having refused to take the oath of allegiance to the Polish armed forces, he found himself in solitary confinement. It was at that time that he experienced the presence of God more deeply than at any other time in his life. 'It was worth being in prison for the sense of God's nearness,' he said. Later he was transferred to a mental hospital, in order that his system of thinking might be 'corrected'. Even then his mind was wonderfully protected and he never lost his sanity, nor indeed his Christian convictions.

At the end of the day, of course, there is nothing that can separate us from God's love if we belong to Jesus Christ. If it is a question of martyrdom then, like Stephen, our face can shine like the face of an angel. Not because there is anything special about us, but because God answers the prayers of those who pray for us and gives special grace to endure. Because of what Christ has done for us, we are protected from God's just judgement on our sins when we die, and we are granted the privilege of the resurrection of the body. From that point of view we are better off in the next life, wonderfully protected by God's presence. It has been well said that you cannot know how to live until you know how to die. To know God's protection as a result of prayer throughout life, at its end and beyond, must be the ultimate experience. Assurance of God's ability to keep us from every kind of danger gives the confidence we need for life in the twentieth century. Never has there been a time when man feels more exposed to physical and spiritual danger. The horrors of terrorism, the police state, drug addiction and AIDS stalk by day and by night, but 'he who dwells in the shelter of the Most High, who abides in the shadow of the Almighty, will say to the Lord, "My refuge and my fortress"' (Psalm 91:1).

Prayer

Almighty God, you are our hiding place. At those times when we are afraid we will trust in you and not be afraid. Thank you that you know all about the dangers of this present life and are well able to preserve our lives. When suffering comes, help us to use it as a blessing when we look to you for your sustaining grace, through Jesus Christ who, for the joy that was before him, endured the cross, scorning its shame and is now seated at your right hand in glory. Amen.

12

Power Signs

I doubt that anyone would disagree with the statement that if we want power in the church we must also have prayer in the church. When Jesus prayed: 'Father, glorify your name,' there was the sound of thunder as a voice came from heaven, and when the early church met together to pray, the place where they were praying was shaken. We wonder today whether when we pray there should be similar evidences of the power of God. So often it is the opposite. The prayer time seems to lack any sense of the power of God. There are no signs following.

There is a fascination about power today, both inside and outside the church. The emphasis on power in the church probably has as much to do with the emphasis on it in the world around us. We are in danger of being governed by the attitude of the world—something which Paul carefully warned us against. Why is there so much interest in power today? And what is the evidence of God's power and his presence among us? These are important questions because we need to have the right expectation of the effects of prayer. As we think about this subject, we need to remind ourselves that God often

71

suprises his people. It is clearly not wrong to try to indicate what answers we expect to our prayers, but it is unwise to limit our expectations of what the Lord can do. He has a wonderful capacity for surprising us by demonstrations of his power.

There are many reasons for the current interest in the power of God, but two stand out. Christians today have become keenly aware of the power of the media. We recognize that the media are able to influence the thinking of millions of people and be the principal trend-setters. Through their channels we are constantly reminded of various forms of human power. We are impressed by the achievements of political, scientific, technological or intellectual power. There is also fresh fascination over spiritual power. Without the knowledge of God and experience of his power, society is acutely aware of the limits of its own resources and seeks for spiritual ones. We are not surprised, therefore, at the growing interest in Eastern religions, spiritism and the occult. Acutely aware of this scenario, the church is strongly tempted to imitate the world in its quest for power: the church must be seen to have spiritual power; the place of prayer must shake if the world is to wake up to God's power. We are tempted to pitch the battle for the attention of the world at the same level. The church must have its share of the media too, but for the wrong reasons so often.

The second reason is related to this, namely that the church seems to be powerless at the present time. In recent years all the major denominations, except the Baptist, have suffered a severe loss of membership, while the more demonstrative Christian groups are making a significant appeal to society. I am not suggesting that this appeal is inappropriate, but it does serve to emphasize the current lack of concern for truth for its own sake. At the same time there is a rapid move away from linear thought, making a rational presentation of the Christian messsage less relevant. Contemporary society tends to respond more to physical and emotional stimuli than it did a generation ago, with less regard for the validity of such movements and whether they represent the true pulse of spiritual life. 'Power is all that matters,' they say. 'If people have plugged into God's power then they have discovered reality.' But the dangers of simply responding to the media rather than the message are obvious.

It is little wonder, therefore, that there is great concern in the church today for power and that the Lord should have greater visibility. This lies behind much of the current interest in signs and wonders and the healing ministry of the church. Certainly there is a need for a greater demonstration of God's power in the world today, but it would be foolish to conclude that if believers do not shake in the Spirit, or are not slain in the Spirit, God has not answered prayer. If there is an absence of miracles, do we conclude there is an absence of power? God's power is sometimes undemonstrative, unseen and silent. If we judge everything on the evidence of the seen, we can easily misconstrue the power of God.

The power of God's presence is many things, but there is a reality about his presence that is unmistakable to the believer. It is something that comes by no other means than Christian prayer. God chooses in his sovereignty how he will display his power in response to prayer. On occasions the place where Christians pray *is* shaken—even if not literally (though I have heard of one report of a physical shaking). When the power of God is at work, those things that imprison the human soul are unlocked, giving the freedom to live as God intends. In the great battle with the evil forces of darkness, demons are driven out and captives are released through prayer.

I remember talking to an elderly Christian worker, much experienced in prayer, who shared her delight in the conversion of an eighty-three-year-old woman in one of her Bible study groups. On finding Christ, this octogenarian immediately asked help for her son who had been gripped with agoraphobia for thirty years. He started out with the prospect of a brilliant career in the legal profession, only to be dogged by agoraphobia, making it impossible for him to work. As a result of prayer over a period of time, this man was gradually released from his fear and is now back at work making a fine contribution, both as a lawyer and a Christian. 'Whenever the fear came on him,' she said, 'I used to pray quietly for him until it subsided again.'

There is also that unseen work of God convincing men and women of their sin. When the fear of God comes on somebody they become acutely aware of their shortcomings. Once again the message of the church about forgiveness of sin carries with it authority and power. The death of Christ seems immediately relevant and there is reconciliation with God. The staggering mercy of God is grasped as people are overwhelmed by the depth of God's love. From that place of spiritual understanding, there is a steady, quiet work of the Spirit of God, giving understanding of the Scriptures and a matching growth in spiritual wisdom and moral power. As Paul the apostle prayed for the Ephesians, so we can pray for others that there be an understanding of the height and depth and length and breadth of the love of Christ which passes human knowledge.

Some of the most significant changes in people's lives are in terms of their fresh attitudes, thought patterns and motivations following conversion. Such changes are as significant and miraculous as the more visible demonstrations of God's power in healings and signs and wonders. The New Testament makes it plain that both are important. We need to be careful that we don't estimate the power of God's presence in terms of the 'visibility of the Lord' only. Some of his greatest workings in response to prayer are hidden, secret and invisible. Prayer is always answered, even if it is not immediately evident. If we pray, we have been heard, whatever the evidence around us might suggest. No genuine cry from the people of God goes unheeded. We need to relearn the lesson God gave Elijah. The Lord was dramatically present on Mount Carmel coming down from heaven with fire. There is a place for that today too. Some believe quite genuinely that the fire at York Minster came down from heaven in answer to prayer for the spiritual state of the Church of England. Without doubt it has been instrumental in applying the brakes to the doctrinal extravagancies of the Bishops' bench. But then later the Lord was not in the earthquake, wind or fire, but in the still small voice. It was an important lesson for Elijah, and for many Christians today.

Prayer

You know our great longing that you would open the heavens and come down among us by your great power. Thank you for promising never to leave your people. Forgive us when we judge your power more by what we see than what we believe. Help us to walk more by faith and less by sight, and drive out the unbelief that limits our expectations of your power. For you, Lord, are able to do far more than we ask or think and to you be the glory always. Amen.

13

The Prayer of Faith

How do we continue praying when things that are clearly
God's will have not happened? For example, when we
pray for laws to be changed; for churches to be started in
areas where there are none; for increasing maturity in
believers; for the hungry to be fed; refugees to be cared
for, but these prayers don't appear to be answered. The
short answer is faith. The writer to the Hebrew Christians said that whoever comes to God must believe that
he exists, and is the rewarder of those who seek him. He
also added that without faith it is impossible to please
him. But what is faith? Faith is waiting for the promises
of God to come true. What God has promised he will
certainly do in his own time and way. Has he not promised to release the prisoners and bring in a kingdom of
righteousness?

Abraham was able to keep praying for many years
because God had promised him a son and heir. The
Bible said he hoped against hope. Everything pointed in
the opposite direction. Both he and Sarah were old and
she was well past child-bearing age. Nevertheless he believed God, and in the end God honoured his faith and
gave him a son and heir. The prayer of faith does not

give up. There is such a thing as the gift of faith.

When the Lord Jesus taught his disciples to have 'faith in God', he told them that if they believed that they would receive what they had asked for, then they had already received it. He did not imply that it would be received overnight. In the context of Mark 11:24, after the cursing of the fig tree, it is arguable that Jesus is talking about the overthrow of Judaism by Christianity. This was achieved over an extended period by the first generation of Christians. Such was their conviction that Jesus Christ would build his church and nothing would be able to prevent it, they kept on praying to that end. Their prayers were amply answered.

But what about something more specific? Are we any different from Abraham? We need to return to the thought of the gift of faith. God is able in a special way to give the gift of faith, enabling us to believe that something is his will. Those who receive it are able to say by faith that something will take place before the event. It would be wrong to assume that such faith is always given in one instalment. It usually arises as the fruit of prayer over a period of time. A growing conviction comes that something very specific is indeed God's will. This fuels prayer. The prayer of faith is born.

A Bible college student who was convinced that she should visit China during her holidays was asked what her plan was concerning the finance involved. She was many hundreds of pounds short of the required target, and the deadline for paying for her trip was but a few days away. She declared that she had no other plan, save the conviction that God would supply, since he had so clearly indicated that to go to China was his will. In one sense she already had the money, in another sense she was still short. Within a matter of days she received through the mail from unexpected sources cheques amounting to the figure required. God's provision caused quite a stir among her friends.

Recently I heard of a similar expression of faith when a university lecturer declared that he believed he would be appointed to a particular post. The possibility seemed remote—especially since the interviews for the post were held during his absence from the country. But the actual appointment was not made. Instead fresh interviews were arranged on a date when he could be available. The circumstances gave rise to his conviction and the prayer of faith. I need hardly add that he was appointed, but not only that, he had professorial status thrown in too! He was a good candidate for the post, but his belief that he would get the job was more than a hunch.

In James 5 we are told that the prayer of faith will save the sick man. It does! Not that that always means physical recovery, but always there is a feeling of God's peace and a restoration of confidence in God's love. Prayer puts the total situation firmly into God's hands. He knows what is best for his servant. In this case it is the faith, not so much of the individual, but of those who minister to him with prayer. They are confident God answers prayer and their faith brings healing to the sick man. Answers to prayer are not always due to personal faith. Others can believe for us. In this way we can encourage one another to believe and minister to each other when the capacity to believe God for something specific has dwindled. Answers to prayer are not due so much to the greatness of our faith, as to the greatness of God's love and faithfulness. The important thing is that in times of sickness or trouble we bring the circumstances to God in prayer and trust in him. All he looks for is a heart that trusts in a great God, with whom nothing is impossible.

In a similar way, J.O. Fraser, working with the Lisu

people in the 1930s on the Chinese-Burma border, was able to inspire others to pray for something which he believed would happen if they shared his conviction. He was convinced that God wanted him to ask friends in England to pray for 100 Lisu families to believe in Christ. He was as specific as that and his conviction about the matter inspired many back in England to pray for many years to that end. The gift of faith helps us to persevere in prayer, whether we possess it or others possess it for us.

Elijah the prophet believed God's promise that the drought, which had come in judgement on God's people, was to end. He told Ahab to get ready for the coming storm and on Mount Carmel, when his servant reported that there was no sign of the rain clouds, he told him to go and look again seven times, believing that God would keep his promise and that rain was on the way. It was only on the seventh occasion that a cloud like a man's hand appeared rising out of the sea. That was evidence enough that a great rain storm was on its way. In a similar way, the first family among the Lisu that turned to Christ guaranteed that ninety-nine more would follow in its train. And they did!

The experience of praying in faith for the realization of something that God has either declared in his word to be his will, or shown to be so through evidences for faith that are clearly recognized by a Christian, creates a quiet confidence in God that is not easily ruffled. Such confidence perseveres in prayer and can take plenty of setbacks on the way to proving that God is faithful in his work and always answers prayer. We need to covet the gift of faith more than we do. It is one of the precious gifts of the Holy Spirit.

Prayer

We thank you, O Lord, for the gift of faith, whether it is received by an individual or the church. Teach us to persevere in prayer and encourage us in the same by bestowing this gift to believe so that your will may be prayed through to reality, and that quiet confidence in your ability to do what you promise may characterize your people, to your honour and glory. Amen.

14

Prayer and the Laying on of Hands

One of the basics to be widely understood by the early
church was the practice of the laying on of hands (Hebrews 6:1–2). In many denominations, the laying on of
hands is limited to ordination or the commissioning of
Christian workers. But ministry with the laying on of
hands has a much wider use.

In daily life there is something very meaningful about
touch. Physical contact communicates love. The hand on
the shoulder of a discouraged friend can bring identifi-
cation with his situation and maybe even sufficient
strength to overcome a problem. It conveys concern and
the willingness to help. The greater the person in our
eyes the more significant is the gesture.

God has given us the ministry of the laying on of hands
to bring near his presence. This is particularly so in the
healing ministry. When we lay hands on the sick in the
name of the Lord we bring to them a fresh sense of his
love. Because of his own agony on the cross, Jesus is no
stranger to the discomfort and loneliness of sickness. By
the ministry of the laying on of hands Jesus draws near
both to heal and to give peace. This can be effective in
the privacy of the home or as part of liturgical worship

during a communion service. The practice is increasingly common in churches, faith often being encouraged by reporting answers to prayer following previous healing services.

The ministry of exorcism is one situation where the laying on of hands should not be used, since we read nowhere in Scripture that Jesus laid hands on those who were demon possessed. Rather he commanded the demons to leave. He used his authority over them and drove them out. We likewise need to minister to those who are demon possessed commanding the evil spirits to leave in the name of the Lord.

It would appear that in the New Testament, the laying on of hands had a wide use. Sometimes the practice was used in praying for believers to receive the fullness of the Holy Spirit. Following the example of the apostle Paul, the early church recognized those who had not received the Holy Spirit in fullness and looked into the matter. As with the believers at Ephesus, if there had been an absence of necessary teaching, then it was explained that the Lord Jesus is the baptizer with the Holy Spirit. The laying on of hands was used to confirm the faith of believers and assure them of acceptance with God. Being right with him, there was nothing to stop the Holy Spirit flooding their hearts with the new life. Sometimes, although clearly not always, this experience was accompanied by speaking in tongues. The point is that the laying on of hands does symbolically convey something. The Anglican confirmation service highlights this. Once the candidate has confirmed his personal faith in Christ there is nothing to prevent him being filled with the Spirit. The anointing of the Holy Spirit is therefore symbolized to him by the laying on of the bishop's hands calling for a response of faith. While little may happen at the time due to the solemnity of the occasion, many have experienced a fresh joy in the Lord or later spoken in tongues in private.

In Old Testament sacrificial ritual the priests laid their hands on the goat to be made the sin offering on the Day of Atonement, symbolizing the placing of the people's sins on the animal, which could only lead to one thing, namely death. When ministers lay hands on believers, they symbolize the conferring of God's free gift of right-eousness, which can only lead to one thing, namely fresh life in the Spirit. In both cases it is God who acts, con-veying either the curse or the blessing. This was dramati-cally summed up when Jesus died on the cross. There the Lord laid on him the iniquity of us all, as Isaiah the prophet explained it. He was made sin for us. Sin was actually laid on him, which could only lead to death. This was accompanied by physical darkness and spiritual darkness when Jesus cried, 'My God, my God, why have you forsaken me.' But since Christ was also fully right-eous, death could not hold him and he arose on Easter day when eternal life burst out of the grave.

To lay hands, therefore, on believers, brings both assurance of sins forgiven and the bursting out of new life in the power of the Holy Spirit. This takes different forms according to the temperament and disposition of believers. If a particular expectation is given, then understandably that phenomena will appear. The im-portant thing is not the emotional experience but the spiritual assurance of knowing that we are children of God. The Spirit bears witness with our spirit that it is so.

In the early church people's call from the Lord to Christian ministry was confirmed by the church with the laying on of hands. Both the first deacons and the first missionaries received the laying on of hands to remind them that those the Lord calls he also equips. Their ex-pectation of his working through them was thereby

COME INTO HIS PRESENCE

raised. As they responded to this tangible form of ministry, so they were freshly filled with the Holy Spirit. We must assume that in each case there was a faith response to the symbol. This is the object of sacraments. For example, we are strengthened by Christ in the communion service only as we receive the symbols of his love, the bread and the wine, by faith. There is nothing inherently powerful about those elements nor does the laying on of hands convey the power of the Holy Spirit automatically. The Lord, however, understood very clearly the value of symbols.

Those for whom prayer has been offered with the laying on of hands speak of a sensation of warmth flowing through the body and of peace in the heart. The relief of sharing personal affliction more publicly, and bringing it into the presence of God, is immediate and beneficial. In many cases, of course, the release of tension is the key to recovery. How many of our health problems are psychosomatic? They are much more problems of the mind than problems of the body.

Many today see not only payment for sins in the work of the cross, but also healing for our bodies. They point out that Matthew saw in the healing ministry of Jesus, the fulfilment of Isaiah's prophecy, 'He took up our infirmities and bore our diseases' (Matthew 8:17). Without doubt sin in its entirety was laid on Jesus when he hung on the cross, and he triumphed over its consequences by his resurrection. But we do not have an unqualified right to healing of the body before Christ's return, when he will change our present feeble body to be like his own glorious risen body. Although the Lord's healing of our bodies today is wonderful, the sufferings he allows are sometimes more purposeful. The Lord knows that while we may be healed in our body, there is often a long way to go in the healing of our personality. At the end of the day, flesh and blood cannot inherit the kingdom of God. His final plan for the body is in the resurrection. Strength of character rather than strength of body is sometimes his design. None of this, however, should deter us from the healing ministry of prayer with the laying on of hands.

Prayer

Lord, we believe it is your will that we identify those you wish to identify by the laying on of hands. It is your desire to bless all those brought to you in this symbolic way. May they open their hearts to receive your love and be filled with the Spirit. Equip them for your service, restoring the sick and anxious so that they may give thanks to you. We ask this in the name of Jesus. Amen.

15
Prayer and Fasting

Jesus warned his disciples not to fast in such a way as to parade their spirituality before others. Fasting is not a meritorious work to bring down the blessing of God. It is, however, a useful discipline for both demonstrating to God the earnestness of our prayers and deepening our communion with him. Fasting clarifies our thoughts about the spiritual battle in which we are engaged, and our perception of God's will.

After Jesus had revealed the glory of heaven to his special friends on the Mount of Transfiguration, he returned to find his disciples defeated by a case of demon possession. 'Why could we not cast it out?' asked the disciples, after Jesus had done so (Mark 9:28). His reply was that such power only comes through prayer and fasting. From this it would appear that certain evil powers are only dislodged by an intensity of prayer that comes through fasting. This is a mystery, but explains why in deliverance ministry fasting has often been found essential if the Lord's victory over all evil powers is to be shared by those for whom we pray. As in healing ministry, when healing takes place over a period of time, prolonged prayer is essential.

Jesus fasted for forty days and forty nights in the wilderness, and from this he drew the strength to resist the subtle and strong temptations of the devil and stand undefeated before him. No doubt it helped him to see clearly the temptations the devil was laying before him, as well as the spiritual issues that his future ministry would need to settle. He repelled the devil, not simply by prayer and fasting, but also by his meditation on the Scriptures—the message of which was unmistakably clear to him as a result of this spiritual discipline. There are times when we need to take similar action to clarify God's will for our lives.

The other context for prayer and fasting is repentance. True grief for sin in the Old Testament was usually demonstrated by fasting. There was a longing that every sin should be faced and forgiveness received. Nothing is more important than God meeting with us when we repent to give victory over sin, for holiness is the hallmark of God's people. This need not necessarily be for personal sin, but for the sins of either the church or the nation, which also call for repentance. In the Old Testament confession of sin was not so much of personal sin, but of the sins of the nation. We have lost that sense of collective responsibility today. To accompany times of prayer for the nation with fasting is a mark of contrition. How serious do we consider the moral and spiritual decline of the nation? If we really mean business we will be prepared both to pray and fast. God needs to see some determination in the matter. At such times God draws near to his people, recognizing the seriousness of their intentions. It could be that sometimes God withholds his presence for the simple fact that he recognizes that our prayers are superficial and lacking in any real commitment to a change of heart or direction.

Provided fluids are taken, people are able to fast for

very long periods of time. God has a remarkable way of sustaining people through a time of prayer and fasting and, as in other extended times of prayer, the whole experience can be one of spiritual renewal and refreshment. If we wish to experience more of God's presence among his people, we shall have to think again about fasting. It is certainly not a meritorious work. This was the mistake that the Pharisees made, but it does express an earnest desire for God's blessing and help in particular situations. When there was a deep consciousness of sin, the people of God both mourned and fasted. When there was an urgent need for God's rescue, fasting was a feature of their call for help. If there was a keen desire to know the mind of the Lord, then fasting was added to praying. The question arises, 'How serious are our intentions when it comes to our relationship with God?' Are they serious enough for us to fast?

Fasting, like praying, can be insincere. Isaiah quarrels with the people of God because they fasted, outwardly expressing their desire to know God's will, while at the same time quite determined to carry on with their own pleasures and lifestyle. If fasting is viewed as some kind of formula for automatic blessing from God, then we shall see no blessing. Fasting, like praying, is all a matter of our relationship with God. It is altering for a while our priorities. It is placing spiritual concerns above immediate physical concerns. It is a confession that our spiritual life is more important than our physical life. We wish to increase our spiritual appetite by denying the appetite of our bodies.

Fasting helps us to increase the spiritual intensity of our relationship with God. We gain a fresh taste for the things of the Spirit. It helps to tune our ear to his voice, especially if we include meditation on the Scriptures. In the midst of a noisy world we begin to hear the silence of eternity. God can sharpen for us the spiritual issues that face us as we think about our home life, church responsibility and work situation. It was when Peter was on the roof top in Joppa praying and fasting that he received one of the most significant visions of his life. Was the apostle Paul similarly caught up to the third heaven during a time of prayer and fasting? If we need a fresh vision from God of himself and his work, then we may well need to take time to fast.

Others point out that fasting is necessary because there is just not enough time for all the praying that should be done. Certainly if our complaint is that we do not have enough time to pray, then to go without a meal in order to have more time to do so is bound to be rewarding. The Bible seems to say that this is one way to gain God's attention. But if we do, we may find God putting his finger on certain things in our lives which require some attention if our relationship with him is to go further. If something has spoilt that relationship, we do well to heed his exhortation: 'Return to me with all your heart, with fasting, with weeping, and with mourning' (Joel 2:12). If fasting helps us to find our way back to God, then we should do it. It may be what is needed for our relationship with God to go deeper.

Prayer

How seriously do we take our relationship with you, O Lord our God? We neither fast and mourn over our sins nor fast and pray over our ways. Give us a deeper desire for your righteousness in our lives and in our land. May we find grace to fast and pray so that we might go deeper into your will, through Jesus Christ our Saviour who fasted forty days and forty nights in the wilderness. Amen.

16

In Secret

There is another area of life where we must not parade ourselves. As Christian people we are not called to justify ourselves before others. 'Vengeance is mine,' says the Lord. 'I will repay' (Romans 12:19). How easy it is, however, to hit back when we have been wounded, especially if it is a matter of injustice. There are few things harder to bear than a miscarriage of justice. It is hard to take being misunderstood and misrepresented, but this is just the kind of situation where we need to be in the secret place enjoying Christ's presence.

In teaching about prayer, Jesus commended the secret place to us. He taught that our heavenly Father sees in secret. If, therefore, we go privately to him about some grievance, we can be sure that he will honour us and in due course vindicate us. If that does not happen in this life, we can be sure that it will in the next and on the last day when he returns to judge the world with righteousness.

Gethsemane was the Lord's secret place. He often went there to pray. It was therefore natural to go there just prior to the events of the cross, the greatest travesty of justice the world has ever seen. Without doubt, the discipline and control necessary for facing the Sanhedrin and Pontius Pilate was obtained in the garden. It was an intense battle not only to come to terms with the will of God, but also the miscarriage of justice it would involve. Great drops of sweat like blood fell from the brow of the Lord Jesus. Can we imagine it will be any easier for us? The temptation will be not to flee to the place of prayer, but to rush to our own defence. There is, however, a quiet strength in being silent before our enemies. 'A quiet answer turns away wrath,' as the proverb goes. It has also to be said that prayer may well help us to see that we are not entirely in the right and that there are some grounds for criticism or misunderstanding. The place of prayer has been the secret of many a Christian leader's strength, especially when the lead given is misunderstood.

Hudson Taylor, the founder of the China Inland Mission (known today as the Overseas Missionary Fellowship), did not wish to draw away the giving of Christians from other worth-while causes when he founded the Mission. He preferred rather to move men through God, by prayer alone. He would make the needs of the Mission known to God in the secret place. As God met the needs of himself and his family, as well as his fellow workers, there was a fresh testimony to the living God. How could he doubt that God cared and would likewise vindicate him? Hudson Taylor and the early missionaries were often misunderstood by fellow missionaries and Christians for their radicalism and simple lifestyle. But the misunderstandings on the whole were overcome by prayer. As Christ's presence was sought, so they received the strength he displayed at his public trial. Christ saw no need to justify his actions before men. Hudson Taylor knew what God had called him to do, and that was sufficient. If he obeyed God, he could leave the consequences with him. But a word of caution is needed here.

Evangelical Christians who have rightly stressed personal salvation and individual guidance, need to remember too the role of the church. We are saved by God's grace from individualism to belong to the people of God. We need therefore to be open to corporate guidance and God's vindication of the church as a corporate body. We need to be willing to submit our personal guidance to that of the church. We may be tempted to stand our ground over an issue that is in reality a matter of opinion rather than truth. The issue would be better handled by the church with the support of the prayers of the corporate body. We need the support of others, and to avoid a false martyrdom. We are not called to stand for Christ and his righteousness alone. The church too must pray in secret and learn to support its members in this way.

There is something very beautiful about praying for the persecuted church. We stand shoulder to shoulder with our brothers and sisters in places like Russia and China, praying that God will vindicate his servants in prison. Their freedom becomes our freedom. Their joy is our joy, for we know the secret of their deliverance. We should be grateful to Canon Michael Bourdeaux and the work of Keston College, which researches the conditions in Russia and other countries behind the Iron Curtain for Christian leaders. The ministry of prayer that has resulted is only equalled by the prayer for Christians in China. God has not only answered prayer, but openly vindicated many who have waited patiently for him.

There is more we can do if someone criticizes or ill-treats us. We can ask for grace to heap 'burning coals on their heads'. If we do not repay evil for evil, but rather show love, words of self-justification or defence are not necessary. Our actions arising from prayer for our opponents will speak for themselves.

It is reported that a Red Guard during Chairman Mao's Cultural Revolution loved nothing better than to taunt the Christians and make life difficult for them. His excessive zeal for the revolution drove his wife out of her mind. Her life was reduced to that of an animal, abandoned by her husband and fed once a day like a dog. He kept her unwashed and unkempt in a small room. One of the Christian women asked his permission to nurse her, which was granted. Gradually the woman was restored to sanity and became a Christian. Her husband had nothing further to say against the Christians. 'Do not be overcome by evil, but overcome evil with good' (Romans 12:21).

Prayer

We thank you, our heavenly Father, that you see us in the secret place of prayer. Give us grace to resist the temptation to justify our actions before men. May we leave you to vindicate your people in your own way and in your own time. Pour into our hearts that most excellent gift of love that in loving our enemies we may walk in the steps of your son, our Lord Jesus Christ. Help us not to be overcome by evil, but to overcome evil with good, for the glory of your name. Amen.

17
Silent Prayer

Not many of us have spoken to kings or presidents, but we have all had that experience of being in the presence of someone in greater authority. We respect them and choose our words carefully. We are unusually silent for fear of causing offence. How strange then, that many of our prayer times are without silence. Are we over-familiar with God? From one point of view we do not need to choose our words carefully. Jesus taught us to call on God as our heavenly Father. The Spirit draws out from our hearts the response 'Abba', the equivalent being 'Daddy'. But on the other hand we should not be rash with our words, for we are addressing God. If we were more silent in God's presence, we might find that fewer words are used, but more telling ones.

An important part of prayer is not what we say to God, but what he says to us. God speaks through his word, the Bible, but he also speaks in the quietness. The Spirit of God can speak to our hearts and help us to meditate on God's character. The contemplation of God's greatness and what he can do becomes to us a living word, a commentary on our situation and a guide to our prayers. How important it is that we learn to listen to God in the stillness of his presence. This does not come easily to us today for we have grown so used to living with a background of noise. Some are even frightened of silence.

It is commonplace these days to have 'Open to God' meetings. I like the title, since it means that we are trying to listen to what he has to say about our lives and the direction of our local church. There is a danger here, of course, lest we open our minds to spirits other than the Holy Spirit. We may believe we can discern between the two, but Paul gives instructions concerning the use of the gifts of the Spirit in the local church because he sees the danger is a real one. He teaches us to test the spirits. He stresses the importance of interpreting the message spoken in tongues, and the weighing of prophecies. If there is to be much of the Spirit then there must be much of the word. Word and Spirit go together. The Spirit's message is rational, intelligent, sensible – indeed the wisdom of God. What the Spirit is saying to the church can be verbalized and checked against Scripture. The Spirit never contradicts the word of God. The message may stretch our faith, but that is another matter.

If we plan to listen to God's voice then it is important first to tune in to God by reading Scripture and meditating silently. We are then likely to hear more reliably what the Spirit is saying. We listen to the Spirit not only through what is spoken. The Holy Spirit has a wonderful way of reordering our thoughts, searching our hearts and showing us the way ahead. The importance of such times cannot be over-emphasized. Christians hear a voice unbelievers never hear. The world may see the results without recognizing the source of divine guidance.

The devil will do his best to interrupt such intimacy with God. We will find that there are disturbances from without, and where there are those Christians who have not been delivered from past contact with the occult, there may even be manifestations of demons within. At very least, the devil will do his best to crowd our lives with noise and keep us from the silence of eternity. As was once wisely said, 'Beware of the barrenness of a busy life.' Some of us give God little opportunity to re-order our lives.

There is a wonderful healing power about being in the presence of God. We sense the stillness when he has drawn near. We realize again that he is the mighty Creator and we are his creatures. He comes to us as the Lord and we are his servants waiting for his commands. God is at the centre of our worship. The Christian church has too easily sold out to the personality-cult and unwittingly diverted attention from the Lord. Great sensitivity in leading worship and times of prayer is needed to ensure that there is true communion with God. Silent prayer has a powerful place in this, and perhaps more powerful than some of us have discovered. If we learn to be quiet more often we might hear the praise of creation and the heavens declaring the glory of God more readily. It would put our praying into perspective. It would lift us up to greater heights of praise as well as humble us to realize in whose presence we are. The privilege of prayer would become clearer to us.

Prayer

O Lord, in our busy, noisy world, help us to find time to be quiet in your presence. May we share with you the silence of eternity and drop your still dews of quietness on our anxious hearts until we discover your love with freshness. Speak, Lord, in the silence while we wait on you, and give us faith and courage to obey what you say, for the extension of your kingdom through Jesus Christ our Lord. Amen.

18

Dark Patches

Many years ago my wife and I were on holiday in the
Lake District. Late one night we took a walk, and it was
one of those overcast nights when the darkness was deep
indeed. And yet we were not afraid. We had one another
for company and we were reminded that darkness and
light are the same to God. What a difference it makes to
the darkness if you are in the right company.

So it is with God's presence. There must be few people
who do not know the line, 'Though I walk through the
valley of death, I will fear no evil.' Death is a very deep
darkness to those who do not know the living God.
God's presence helps us to go through the dark tunnels
of life. These can be both mysterious and difficult. We
know the promise of God, 'I will never leave you or
forsake you,' but sometimes it seems that he does. Not
even prayer seems to help during those times.

The Lord Jesus, however, is no stranger to this experience. There was a time when he faced deep darkness,
when on the cross bearing our sin, he cried out in agony,
'My God, my God, why have you forsaken me?' For the
first time in his life he felt forsaken by God. Gone was
the sunshine of his Father's love. There was no sense of

his presence in the desolation, but he knew that his Father was still there. Sometime later he said, 'Father, into your hands I commend my spirit.' When feelings desert us, faith holds us. We may not feel the nearness of God's presence, but we know that he is still with us.

At such times we are called to speak words of faith. Paul in his reflections on missionary service gives us the key to people stepping into the presence of Christ. In Romans 10, he warns us not to climb up to heaven to find God's presence, for that is to bring Christ down. The incarnation, however, is a fact of history. Neither are we to go down to the place of departed spirits, for that is to bring Christ up. The resurrection likewise is a piece of hard history. Aware then of the evidences for faith, what are we to do? We are not only to believe in our heart, but to confess with our lips that Jesus is Lord. The very confession of our faith brings near the presence of Christ.

In times of spiritual darkness, therefore, in our prayers we need above all words of faith. We need to say with full conviction 'Jesus is Lord' and look for his deliverance. In due time he will bring us out of the dark tunnel and into the sunshine once again. For some it can be a very long tunnel of depression. It is never easy to pray at such times. It is sometimes easier if others pray with us. It is certainly not the time to give up praying, nor to forsake the prayer meeting. Others can help us through the darkness by their faith and prayers. It may be that professional help is needed—some of us by nature are more depressive than others and respond negatively to the circumstances of life—but how many of us have been wonderfully helped through by prayer.

There is a darkness that cannot be thrown off without special ministry. There is no doubt that the devil can throw a cloud over our prayer times. We feel oppressed and unable to get through to God. Sometimes there is more to the oppressive atmosphere than satanic attack, but we need to recognize that this is one of the devil's weapons to discourage us in the matter of prayer. He knows that if he succeeds, then he has done more than stop us praying; he has rendered us ineffective. For without Christ's presence in our lives we can neither live his life nor do his works. The important thing is to remember that the darkness cannot shut out the Lord, for he has promised to be with us to the end of the age.

When we are going through a dark passage in our lives, especially when there is no apparent reason for it, the discipline of prayer is a great help. Every time we have our prayer time, we are in effect making a fresh confession of faith. We are resisting the temptation to look to other sources for the way out. It has been well said that a Christian is at his most vulnerable point when he is either on a spiritual high or a spiritual low. In both situations the temptation is to let go of our relationship with God, for we can easily be self-confident when we are up, and doubting when we are down. Instead we need a steady walk with God through life, knowing that he never changes and can be relied on to see us through any situation however difficult.

The Bible can help us greatly at such times. So many of the writers went through times of great darkness. They too had to speak words of faith. Micah the prophet knew that the dark days in which he lived were due to the nation's sin with which he identified. But he believed God would have mercy on him. 'Though I sit in darkness, the Lord will be my light. . . He will bring me out into the light; I will see his justice' (Micah 7:8–9, NIV). He could cope with what is often the hardest part of going through the darkness, the taunts of those who deride our trust in God. John Bunyan in his *Pilgrim's Progress* put these marvellous words of faith into Christian's mouth when he was almost overthrown in the struggle with Apollyon: 'Do not gloat over me, my enemy! Though I have fallen, I will rise.'

Whatever the darkness, we need to remember that the darkness is as light to God (Psalm 139:12). Just as we cannot hide from God in the darkness, so the darkness does not hide him from us. We need to echo Micah's words, 'But as for me, I keep watch for the Lord, I wait in hope for God my Saviour; my God will hear me' (Micah 7:7, NIV).

Prayer

Thank you, O Lord, that you are a God for the dark days as well as the days of sunshine and peace. Help us to remember that darkness and light are the same to you. Fill our mouths with words of faith when passing through the dark patches of life. May we never give in to the taunts of those who mock our trust in you, and bring us through again into your marvellous Light, vindicated by your justice and delivered by your power, for the glory of your name. Amen.

19

Freedom in Prayer

There are many reasons why it is difficult to pray. Sometimes there is an oppressiveness about our prayer gatherings that is of our own making. Jesus was most insistent that a proper relationship with God is not possible unless we have a proper relationship with our neighbour. He points out that if we stand to pray and know in our hearts that there is something that a brother has against us, or we have against a brother, we must first go and put that right. This is not an easy matter. Sometimes we try to pray when we know all the time that there is a lack of reconciliation. We judge that we are reconciled with the Father, but we know that we are not to one another. We may long for the freedom of the Spirit in prayer, but he is grieved by the lack of reconciliation. It is impossible to escape our responsibility as a member of the body of Christ. It may be costly, but we cannot ignore the teaching of Jesus. 'You will know the truth, and the truth will make you free,' he said (John 8:32). Freedom comes only when relationships are right.

In opening the channels of our lives for God to work, as we pray, we must be prepared for the Holy Spirit to convince us of sin. There may be the need to ask for forgiveness from one another, as well as from God. We run away from the subject of church discipline, for we see it as a very harsh and condemning exercise, but there is a call in Scripture for Christians to watch over one another. If a fellow believer falls into sin, we are taught to restore him gently. That means at least that we pray for him to repent, and forgive him when the wrong has been confessed. This is not judgemental, but one of the ways in which we care for others. It is foolish to forget that at best the church is a group of sinners. When aware of others' shortcomings, we need to say, 'But for the grace of God, there go I.'

We cannot expect to have a deep sense of the presence of God and the power of the Holy Spirit in our prayer times if there is unconfessed sin and members are not reconciled to one other. If we are secretly nursing grievances or there is jealousy and bitterness, we can only expect tension, oppression and coldness of spirit. Freedom in prayer comes as we are united in Christ, and work together for the coming of his kingdom. If that essential Christian unity is not present, and there is rivalry and a spirit of competition, the Holy Spirit is grieved and has no freedom to work in our hearts dealing with sin, giving repentance, and interceding for God's people according to the will of God.

We can so easily deceive ourselves at this point. We maintain the outward show of prayerfulness, but inwardly there is no peace of heart and mind. We imagine that the problems will go away. While prayer may be our greatest need when relationships in a church or fellowship have been damaged, we cannot avoid the need both to ask for forgiveness and to forgive and forget the hurts caused.

While the church preaches forgiveness of sins and yet fails to openly confess its own shortcomings and live in the joy and freedom of forgiveness, the authenticity of the message will be in doubt. It is part of the deceitfulness of sin that while we openly acknowledge that we are sinners, we are unwilling to confess specific sin. The society that should find it the easiest to say 'sorry' finds itself bound in ·a false respectability as if the days for admitting sin are past. Here lies the lack of freedom in prayer and worship, which is so much a part of many congregations.

The prelude to one of the great revivals among the churches of Korea was one among the missionaries in the late 1930s. A little woman, Miss Aletta N. Jacobsz and her friend Miss Eunice Marais visited Korea for a holiday. They were both from South Africa. Miss Jacobsz was asked to speak to the prayer meetings, which she did with disarming simplicity. She went from Bible verse to Bible verse pointing out specific sins. Whenever anyone confessed himself to be a great sinner he was asked which sins he was confessing! The missionaries discovered that the supposed united mission station had buried away misunderstandings and jealousies, which had to be confessed and put right. The revival thus began. Freedom in prayer came with power and much blessing. Korean friends saw meals go untouched, lights burning all night, weeping and joy. They wondered what the little lady had been saying!

Prayer

Dear merciful Lord, with the hypocrisy that masquerades for respectability, give us grace to acknowledge the grieving of the Holy Spirit and to be reconciled to one another. May we be willing to apologize to those we have hurt, and forgive those who have hurt us; and to confess once again that we are sinners saved by your mercy and grace alone. Set us free, O Lord, to pray together, united in the body of Christ and by your love shown to us on the cross. We ask this for your name's sake. Amen.

20

Responding to God's Voice

There is much discussion today about how people hear God's voice. If we were to put the question to the Old Testament prophets they would reply that the word of the Lord just came, and they knew it. One moment it was not there, the next moment it was. In one sense we do not need to worry about this question, because we have the prophecies written down for us to hear the word of the Lord as we read them. All that is written is the word of God and not just what we hear the Lord speaking to us, as some have suggested. Others who did not see themselves in the prophetic role nevertheless wrote inspired by the Spirit for us to hear the word of the Lord through them also.

When we turn to the New Testament, the prophets, although fewer, claim revelation from God and pass on a specific message to the people of God for their response. They too do not explain how that word came to them, and the church is taught, in any event, to weigh such prophecies against everything else that is known about God through the Scriptures. As individual believers we believe we hear God speaking to us—not in audible tones, but within the heart. The experience defies explanation, and we may sometimes be mistaken. The safeguards are the revelation of God in the Scriptures and the confirmation or otherwise of the church, the body of believers. While we can misconstrue the inner witness of the human spirit to the Spirit of God, on the whole we are hearing God's voice and are not being led astray at all.

In some situations God speaks not only this way, but also visually. Men and women of God receive visions or dreams. They are very much messages from the Lord of deep theological significance. Moses saw the Lord in the burning bush and understood that God is self-sufficient and does not rely on men or nature for his ability to do what he promises to do. Isaiah saw a vision of the Lord in the temple and realized there was a message of atonement to be preached for the blessing of sinners. John the apostle fell down as a dead man when he was confronted with a vision of the Lord Jesus in glory, and needed a word of encouragement to pass on the message to the seven churches.

In every case where God's people have heard the word of the Lord prayer has followed, because when God speaks the natural response is one of prayer. This highlights the importance of the Scriptures in the place of prayer. The two means of grace intertwine and should be used together. To allow time for prayer after the teaching of God's word, whatever the context, can only be a good thing. This is the context for some of the deepest encounters between God and man.

The desire for what I can only call the immediacy of the Lord with his people has led to the acceptance of much that passes for prophecy. The nature of that gift needs careful definition. What is claimed to be prophecy today is more in the nature of an exhortatory message and often is not particularly original. Certainly the incident of predictive prophecy is rare, but that was some-what similar in the New Testament. My point here is that the willingness to be open to a word from the Lord (what evangelicals of a previous generation viewed as an apt application of Scripture to the current situation) is surely a stimulus to praying in the Spirit. It reminds us that hearing God's voice is not an end in itself for the Christian life is meant to be a day-to-day encounter with the Lord and an on-going dialogue about his will and our way through life. It is to walk with God through a life of prayer.

Prayer

We thank you, O God, for the Scriptures by which you speak to your people. May we hear your voice as we read and study the word of God, the Bible. Help us to hear your voice when you choose to speak in other ways through prophecies, visions or dreams, and to respond to what you are saying. We cannot dictate to you how and when you will speak to us, but help us to open our ears and eyes that we might be guided by you in our daily lives, through Jesus Christ our Lord. Amen.

21

Resisting the Devil

Prayer is the activity most hated by the devil. He will do his best to hinder prayer. It is his activity we encounter when all kinds of obstacles are put in the way of our prayer times. It is common experience for a Christian to have his personal prayer life interrupted or hindered, and the corporate life of the church is similarly affected. We need spiritual discernment to realize what is going on. One of the first signs of spiritual decline, both in personal and corporate life, is the dwindling amount of time and attention given to prayer. If prayer is getting squeezed out then we cannot be complacent. Without any further activity the devil has already caused us to become both ineffective in Christian work and insensitive to the will of God. By tempting us to put a low priority on prayer, the devil is trying to rob us of spiritual power and safeguard his own kingdom.

Why does the devil oppose prayer so consistently? As already mentioned, there is a spiritual battle going on as the devil tries to usurp God's power and hold men and women in his sway. The devil is the opponent of all that is good and is bent on destroying life. He tempts men and women therefore away from the good and creative will of God, to do their own thing. They end up with the disillusionment that such living brings. But more important, life as God planned it to be never materialises. In succumbing to the temptations of the evil one, men and women find that life becomes a rather sordid affair. Sin pervades everything once we cease aiming at God's will and glory. However, unbelievers are not easily dislodged from their loyalty to selfishness and sin. It is only as the power of God is brought to bear on men and women that they repent and enter the kingdom of God. It should not surprise us therefore that prayer for evangelism and mission especially comes under attack from the evil one. Only an appreciation of the spiritual battle that is being waged will help us to keep the priority of prayer. Paul perceived that behind the opposition to the gospel lay the spiritual powers of wickedness in the heavenly places, orchestrated by the great opponent himself, the devil. So he encourages us to pray at all times, for nothing less will ensure victory.

The most helpful picture in the whole of Scripture comes in Revelation 12. Here we are introduced to the activity of the evil one as he attempts to swallow up new Christians the moment they have been born again of the Spirit. What an accurate picture this is. How many people who have professed faith in Christ have been quickly drawn aside to other interests or have been persuaded not to seek the counsel and help that they need at that time. Their spiritual growth is effectively hindered. The spiritual battle is portrayed as 'war in heaven'. Michael and his angels are fighting against the Dragon and his. Fortunately for us Michael wins the battle and the Dragon loses his hold on the church. What an encouragement to know that the Dragon is not strong enough to overthrow Michael and his angels. The church is always victorious. Since the good angels are God's servants with a commission to act in the interests of God's people, it is reasonable to suppose that as we pray so the heavenly hosts engage the enemy and weaken his hold on the church. The church for its part, sensing the victory available through Christ, resists the devil and finds he is a defeated enemy. James gives the simple advice: 'Resist the devil and he will flee from you' (James 4:7). Not only are we to resist his temptations to abandon prayer, but also everything else that he conjures up to destroy the church.

In some cases, of course, the devil is not easily shifted. Not that the blame for everything should be laid at his door! We have an unbalanced tendency to do that these days without realizing that other factors are also at work. Some Christians experience real spiritual oppression and depression. While some of this may come from the devil himself, and cannot just be shrugged off without intercessory prayer, such experiences may be related, for example, to physical well-being accompanying normal changes in our bodies, which call for the help of the doctor. To go to the opposite extreme, however, and not use the weapon of prayer to lift spiritual oppression and depression, is a denial of the power of prayer. If lives have been opened to the devil, especially through occult practices, the skilled ministry of exorcism may be required. In these days with the growth of witches' covens and all manner of occult practices, the Church of England is wise to appoint official Diocesan exorcists. An exorcist is called to resist the devil 'in the name of the Lord Jesus Christ' while, at the same time, being wise enough not to attribute to the devil more than the facts warrant.

Some people believe that Christians can never be demon possessed. They hold that since the Lord Jesus broke the powers of the devil on the cross, those who have believed and live beneath 'the power of the blood' are delivered from demon possession and anything that the devil might hurl at us. But there is the warning of the man who drove out a demon, swept his house, made it clean and tidy, only to have it reoccupied again by a whole band of demons worse than the first. Christians are exhorted to be filled with the Spirit and to be taken up with God's will, but where there is compromise and dabbling in the occult there is always the danger of becoming subject to demons once again. For that reason it seems wise when counselling people suffering from spiritual oppression and depression to ask questions concerning their involvement in the occult. There may be a need for prayer ministry to help them resist the devil and escape once again from his clutches. James in his exhortation to resist the devil is talking about submission to the will of God and refers to those who need to draw near to God as 'double minded'. The double minded are those who dally with the devil, pulling back from a wholehearted commitment to the will of God. Our selfish desires often originate with the devil. We need to learn to recognize that and resist him. Prayer, once again, is our most effective weapon.

Prayer

We thank you, O Lord, that your church can always be victorious over her arch-enemy the devil through your risen power. Give us spiritual discernment to recognize his spoiling work and to resist his temptations. Show us that the opposition we experience to the work of your kingdom is part of the great spiritual battle raging in the heavenly places and that we can gain the victory through prayer. So may your will be done on earth as it is in heaven, through Jesus Christ our Lord. Amen.

22

Releasing the Captives

Those who are not Christians would dispute strongly the statement that they are held captive by the devil. For one thing they do not believe in him! They believe themselves to be in control of their own destiny. The truth is, however, that they are captured by him to do his will. Evangelism, therefore, is very much a matter of releasing the power of God to set free the captives. This is done chiefly by teaching the word of God backed up with prayer, making it an effective message in the hearts of those who hear. While most Christians understand the importance of prayer in evangelism, few are convinced enough to spend the time required. If it is true that 'the god of this world has blinded the minds of the unbelievers, to keep them from seeing the light of the gospel of the glory of Christ who is the likeness of God' (2 Corinthians 4:4), why should we think that with a bit of gentle persuasion people will understand the good news?

Evangelism is a supernatural work of God and every conversion is a miracle. The fact that the good news falls on deaf ears has more to do with our neglect of prayer than the relevance of the message. God says by the prophet Ezekiel that he delights 'to be enquired of' by his people concerning the conversion of others. 'I will yield to the plea of the house of Israel and do this for them.' It is God's prerogative to give men and women the precious gift of eternal life. When Jesus said that no one comes to him except the Father draw him, he was acknowledging the same truth. But that does not give us the excuse to lapse into fatalism by drawing the conclusion that this or that person is not chosen to belong to God's people, but rather encourages us to persevere with the longing that others be set free from the evil one.

George Muller, shortly after his own conversion, began to pray for five friends. The first one was converted within a matter of months and another three over the years of his long life. He was no doubt very disappointed that he never saw his fifth friend come to Christ, as this happened shortly after his death. George Muller never gave up praying for his friends.

We wonder why some seem to be more effective in personal evangelism than others. Men like the Reverend E.J. Nash of the Varsity and Public School Camps, or T.S. Mooney of the Crusader Union in Northern Ireland, brought a steady stream of boys to Christ over the years. The secret in both cases has been prayer. Both these men were known to be up early in the morning with prayer lists lying on top of their Bibles, as they interceded for boys they had met. Little wonder, therefore, that one by one they not only came to Christ but grew in their knowledge of him and effectiveness in Christian service.

My own testimony in the matter is that shortly after my own conversion to Christ I was told that the rest of the Bible study group I attended had been praying earnestly for me. Since there were about thirty in the group I concluded that I was 'the greatest of sinners'! I came to appreciate that here lay the secret of a most successful piece of Christian evangelistic work. For I was one among a large number of soldiers who turned to Christ and went forward for full-time Christian work. If we learnt this lesson, how much more effective our evangelistic programmes would be. But too easily we forget what a strong hold the devil has on people.

Jesus once gave an illustration about his power to free people from the devil's clutches. He spoke of the need to bind 'the strong man' before you can enter his house to take hold of his goods. That 'binding' Jesus did on the cross, but we still need to apply the power of the cross to individuals by praying for them. Once people are overwhelmed by the power of Jesus' love, they will surrender their lives to his control. The miracle of the transforming friendship of the Lord Jesus then begins. That transformation is one of the greatest rewards of prayer.

When the Borneo Evangelical Mission workers first heard about the Lun Bawang people of East Malaysia, they were a dying tribe. Drink was a scourge. The infant mortality rate due to parental neglect was causing the tribe to head for extinction. The colonial officials were glad to see the last of them. But then people began to pray for these miserable people. The good news of Jesus Christ was preached. Instead of extinction it was a matter of distinction, as one by one members of the tribe turned in repentance to Christ. Today there is a vibrant church of Lun Bawang people and many have responsible jobs in the community. Their students study in British universities, and challenge British students about their addiction to drink. They know how to escape from the captivity of the devil.

Prayer

Thank you, Lord Jesus, that when you died on the cross you bound Satan and broke his powerful hold on the lives of so many. Help us by prayer to apply the power of the cross to the lives of our friends who do not know you, and to see them set free from sin and its slavery to serve you with the freedom you alone can give, to the praise and glory of your great name. Amen.

23

Helping the Growth

The main task of missionary work is prayer. Some would dispute that, but Jesus taught that the key to the supply of workers for cross-cultural evangelism is prayer. When he had seventy recruits, he turned to them and told them that the harvest was abundant but the workers were few. He went on to explain that the solution to the paucity of workers was prayer. Those engaged in cross-cultural evangelism will also tell you that God does nothing except in answer to the prayers of his people. The current lack of interest, therefore, in praying for missionaries is something those overseas find deeply disturbing. They know their effectiveness depends on the prayers of those at home. Results are achieved, of course, because they themselves pray for the work and encourage new believers to do likewise, but how much more would be achieved if we grasped the importance of praying for missionary work?

When prayer for local evangelism is so inadequate, it is not surprising that prayer for overseas work is even more so. It is difficult to pray for something that is happening thousands of miles away. There are, however, many aids to such prayer. Cross-cultural evangelistic workers send out prayer letters. We need to trust those who write such letters, believing that they are seeing the pattern of God's working on the ground and we are being directed by them in our praying. There is also the help of missionary magazines. Most societies do their best to give helpful background information to assist prayer. In addition to that, there are many prayer conferences giving us the opportunity to listen to those reporting on the situation overseas and to join with others in prayer. As we grow in the Christian life so God brings us into contact with missionaries and helps us to love them by praying regularly for them. If we keep a list of their names and ask the Holy Spirit to assist us in our intercession for them, he will. As we continue in prayer over the years we will discover how much we have been a part of a work thousands of miles away.

Knowing as we do that the Lord Jesus has all authority in heaven and on earth, and nothing is impossible for him, we can pray boldly for the advance of the church, even in the most unpromising situations. Jesus assured us that the gates of hell would not be able to hold out against the advance of the church. So often changes in government have been due as much to the prayers of God's people as power politics. Who can deny that the ascendancy of Deng Xiao Ping in China is an answer to the prayers of God's people over many years for the restoration of the church in that land? Similarly the overthrow of President Marcos in the Philippines, and the victory of President Aquino, with the support of the National Movement for Free Elections (NAMFREL), happened because many Christian churches committed themselves to nights of prayer for the outcome of the elections and the future of their country. Not that those political forces that are sympathetic to the church are always determinative. The rise of Solidarity in Poland undoubtedly helped the church to grow, but its more recent demise has done nothing to deter the church which continues to grow in places like Gdansk where the Solidarity Movement began. Once people have discovered that prayer can alter the direction of history they are not easily persuaded to lessen its priority. British Christians have caught a glimpse of that power at work in the defeat against all the odds of the Sunday Trading Bill in the House of Commons. This was an answer to prayer as much as the outcome of an effective campaign.

One of the privileges of being a Christian is membership in the worldwide church. We accept the privileges and responsibilities of such membership by praying for the church overseas. The apostle Paul prayed for those he had never met, and he could do so because he understood so clearly the universal nature of the church. All those in Christ were his brothers and sisters. He wanted to play his part in the family of God worldwide. We too can come to know national Christians through the reports of missionaries and through our prayers experience fellowship with them. With the growing multi-racial nature of our society we often meet Christians from the lands where missionaries we know are working. This is a great bonus for our praying. We also discover that missionary work is not one way. There are prayer groups in Nigeria praying for God's work in Britain. Nigerian Christians coming to Britain thinking that it is a fully Christian country have been sadly disillusioned. Rather than criticize the church in Britain they have gone back to Nigeria and prayed for the revival of the church in our land. We are acutely aware of the need for revival in our own land and it is a wonderful thing to discover that the church in other lands is praying to that end also.

Praying for missionary work, therefore, is asking God that his own desire to draw people from every ethnic group around the world to himself might become a reality. This is his plan for our world—a multi-racial people redeemed by Christ and living for the glory of God. This is the one and only plan that will truly unite the nations and cross the barriers erected by man in his sin and folly. Prayer is therefore one of the greatest contributions we can make to worldwide peace and racial harmony, especially if we are focusing our prayers on the growth of the universal church. For the church is called to model God's pattern for living to the world. It is meant to be a constant challenge to others of what is possible by the grace of God.

How then should we pray for the overseas Christian worker in an alien culture? We should do so with imagination. Try to put yourself in the other person's shoes. There are new sights to see, foods to taste, customs to observe. This leads to a sense of disorientation commonly called culture shock. But there are also fresh thought patterns to understand, and relationships to be established. It is all too easy for misunderstandings to creep in, and respect for one another to diminish. The truth is that there is hardly an area of life which does not need to be covered by prayer. We need to pray for the physical, mental and spiritual health of those called to work overseas, as the extra demands are real and considerable—especially in the early days of living overseas. Added to all that is the fact that the work will not go uncontested and the devil will do his best to bring it to a swift end. But if the church is to grow around the world, it will only do so as Christian workers are sent overseas by the local church and are prayed for by congregations and personal friends. Paul may have planted the seed of the word of God in Corinth, and Apollos watered it by his teaching ministry, but it was God who gave the increase. And God will, if we ask him. Just as he will help those who have left their homelands to help the growth of the church worldwide. Can those overseas say of their situations, as Paul did of his, 'I know that through your prayers and the help given by the Spirit of Jesus Christ, what has happened to me will turn out for my deliverance' (Philippians 1:19). The situation turned out for the deliverance of others too as they watched Paul and Silas in prison and were attracted to their God. No other single factor contributes to the growth of the church as much as prayer.

Prayer

Widen our horizons, O Lord, as we pray for the universal church and help us to understand that our prayers make a difference to its growth. The harvest is abundant, waiting to be reaped for your glory, but the workers are so few. We pray that you will send out fresh workers from our congregations and give us grace to follow them faithfully with our prayers. We ask it that your great plan to draw all nations together in Christ might be fulfilled through Jesus Christ, our Lord. Amen.

24

Prayer Without Ceasing

One of the most remarkable missionaries was a man
called Haldane of Morocco. He worked for forty years in
that land without seeing a single profession of faith in
Christ. Wisely he saw the strategic importance of children's work and spent considerable time telling them
about the Lord Jesus. He was a man of great faith and
much prayer, and there was a circle of friends who
prayed regularly for his work. But it was in fact his suc-
cessors who saw the significant answers to their prayers.
Shortly after his death there was a considerable turning
to Christ and quite a number of clear professions of
faith. God always answers prayer, but sometimes we
have to wait a long time for the answers to come.

We have to admit, though, it *is* difficult to continue
when prayer is not answered. Here our faith is tested
severely, but we know as the apostle John put it in his
letter, 'If we ask anything according to his will he hears
us. And if we know that he hears us in whatever we ask,
we know that we have obtained the requests asked of
him' (1 John 5:14–15). Faith believes that and learns to
wait for the answer.

Elijah was a man who knew the same truth. In the

days of King Ahab he prayed for rain knowing that God was going to send some. When his servant on Mount Carmel returned to say that there was no sign of rain on the horizon, Elijah made him go back and look again. This was repeated seven times and on the seventh occasion there was a small cloud the size of a man's hand in the sky. That was enough for Elijah. He told the king to get ready for the rain. As we continue to pray about something, we would be wise to look, as it were, for any sign of rain.

Sometimes we don't have the eyes to see what God is doing. We fail to notice that attitudes are changing, or that Christians are growing, and that God is quietly yet steadily at work preparing his people for fresh leadership and advance. Too many of us despise the day of small things. We need to learn that God will fulfil his purposes in his own way and in his own time.

We also assume that we will be the ones who will play the principal role in the coming of God's kingdom in the lives of those for whom we pray. We need to be less self-centred. God can use many different circumstances and people to speak to others. After praying for nearly thirty years for a close relative, I discovered that she had a real interest in Christian biography and assumed that this would lead to an opportunity to explain the meaning of a personal faith in Christ. I found that she had responded to an advert offering a free copy of *The Way of Freedom* and this was the tool that God used to bring her to faith in Christ. The important thing is not how God answers prayer, but that he does in the end.

Abraham was a man who persisted in prayer. In so doing he discovered that life holds some surprises. We read in Genesis 18 about his persistent prayer for the cities of Sodom and Gomorrah. He was anxious for God to spare the cities for the sake of the godly few living in them. In the end God did not spare the cities. The surprise was that only his own relatives living in the city were right with God and were therefore delivered from judgement. Sometimes we find it hard to believe that the situation is as serious as it is. We underestimate the evil in the world and the stubborn and unrepentant nature of men's hearts. Such considerations, however, should make us not less persevering but more, as well as urgent, like Abraham, that in his wrath God would remember mercy and rescue our relatives from judgement.

Of one thing we can be sure. God always answers prayer. As the friends of Haldane in Morocco discovered, if God doesn't answer in the present generation he will surely do so in the next. This perspective can help up to persevere. It is helpful to read the testimony of Christian leaders from churches that were started less than 100 years ago. How the early missionaries must have despaired of head hunters, witch doctors or Buddhist priests whose grandsons today are the pastors and evangelists of the churches which were only dreams not many years ago.

Sometimes the Spirit of God calls us to stop praying. The burden or concern is lifted, and we sense that God has heard and will answer in due course. It is our part now to wait with expectant faith. Praying friends of Minka Hanskamp and Margaret Morgan, OMF missionaries who were captured by guerrillas in South Thailand some years ago, experienced this. After praying for weeks without ceasing for their release, there was a significant leading of the Spirit of God to stop praying. In the event, the two nurses had been shot as martyrs in the hills not far from Saiburi Christian hospital where they worked, at the time God lifted the burden of prayer in their homelands. He had answered the prayers of his people by taking his servants to be with him in heaven.

Their need for prayer was no more. The Spirit of God, who is the Spirit of intercession, made that clear to God's people. Here is a further call to sensitivity in prayer.

Prayer

Lord Jesus, you taught that men should always pray and not give up. May we persevere in prayer, allowing you to mould our prayers to your will, in the confidence that you always answer us. Make us sensitive to the guidance of the Holy Spirit, then help us to rest in the knowledge that you do all things well. We praise you for your goodness and mercy that follow us all our days. Amen.

25
Recognizing His Presence

Many of us will have gone through that rather disillusioning experience of having been present at a major event and then reading about it in the daily newspaper. Some times you wonder whether you and the reporter attended the same function. The media have their own message to convey. For some the message is the medium. However, a Christian's interest in the world events should be a keen one. The central message of the book of Revelation is that world history is under the control of God. The One who died as the Lamb of God to redeem us, is the One who reigns on the throne on our behalf. At the end of the day history is his story as God rules, or perhaps we should say overrules the nations to achieve his own objectives. In other words, everything has a bearing on the church. The church is the centre of God's purposes. It is therefore a great privilege to belong to God's people and to be chosen by him to be part of 'the holy nation'.

Some Christians say they don't know what to pray about, but against the biblical background there is so much. Dramatic changes in policies and attitudes are brought about as a result of prayer. For many years no one was willing to talk to the African National Congress. Then it seems overnight all are willing to do so. So-called terrorists become negotiators. The winds of change abroad are often brought about by the sovereign work of God's Spirit. Like the prophets in the Old Testament we need to recognize when God is raising someone up to be 'his servant' even when, as in the days of Isaiah, he is like Cyrus who did not acknowledge God, nor realize he was fulfilling God's purposes.

Too often the prayers of God's people are about their own private affairs. They have no vision of God on the stage of world affairs. Any prayer, therefore, that has been made for kings and those in authority has been half-hearted and unbelieving. There is little conviction about its effectiveness. We should be grateful to those Christians who alerted us, for example, to the fact that the government intended to 'hijack our Sunday'. It created the right climate for God to work and stimulated a spirit of prayer across the nation. The defeat of the Sunday Trading Bill surprised the church in Britain, but perhaps did more to awaken it to the power of prayer than any other single event for many years. The church, because of the gift of prayer, holds the key to the destiny of the nations. Not that the church itself has the authority and power to do anything, but it knows the One to whom all authority and power in heaven and on earth has been given. The privilege and potential of intercession are enormous.

During the last world war the churches in Britain were full of people praying for the nation. It was realized that unless God intervened there was no hope of deliverance. The great calm at sea during the battle of Dunkirk was recognized as the merciful hand of God enabling thousands of British troops to evacuate the French coast and get safely home. Similarly, had the German bombers not inexplicably switched their raids from London during the great blitz the country would have been crippled beyond foreseeable recovery. But God intervened, as he has done again and again throughout history to make it clear who in the last analysis rules the nations. It is the eye of faith that can see his hand. And where there is faith there is also prayer. Not everyone is surprised by sudden changes in events, particularly those interceding for the nations. Friends of the church in Cambodia saw the invasion of the Vietnamese troops which brought to an end the appalling reign of terror under Pol Pot as the answer to their prayers.

This was the atmosphere that pervaded the faith of Israel. The Jews were and still are deeply aware that their God is Lord of lords and King of kings and the God of history. The Psalms abound with prayers for deliverance or praises for his great acts in history. For the Jews history moves towards a goal, the coming of the Messiah. Christians share the same faith perspective, while acknowledging his first coming as the Son of God. The cry of the early church was, 'Come, Lord Jesus.' For then justice would reign and the sufferings of the world end in the New Age. This perspective gave substance to many of the prayers of the early church, and should still do so today to ours. For prayer is always a hopeful exercise. It gives fortitude and perseverance against incredible odds. Even when the Christian's cause seems to be lost, there is the conviction that all in fact is not lost. God has yet to have his say in the matter.

When the truths of our faith weaken, so does our prayer life. For prayer is linking what we know about God to our human situation. It is recognizing both that God can transform our human predicament and when he is doing so. History does not just pass by the Christian. He tries to see the mark of God's footsteps across its pages.

Prayer

We acknowledge that you are the Lord of history, and rule over the nations as our sovereign Lord. Help us to read our newspapers and listen to world news with a true perception and not to despair about our world, for you, O Lord, work all things together for the good of your church and people. Ultimately the kingdoms of this world will become the kingdoms of our Lord and Saviour Jesus Christ to his praise and glory. Amen.

26

Love Gifts of Prayer

When the Lord Jesus was on earth he went a long way
beyond the expectation of those who looked to him for
help. 'Don't bother the teacher any more,' a friend said
to Jairus whose daughter had just died. But not long
after, and in spite of the mocking of Jairus' friends, Jesus
brought his daughter back to life again. The apostles
created the same expectation. Peter said to the man
crippled from birth, 'I have no silver and gold, but I give
you what I have; in the name of Jesus Christ of
Nazareth, walk' (Acts 3:6).

In stark contrast, our expectation today of what God
can do for our friends and neighbours is often very low.
When the love and power of God is so great it is sad that
we limit our prayers so much. Jesus taught us that whatever we ask in his name he would do. We need to pray
more in the powerful name of Jesus and bring his authority and power to bear on the many hopeless situations
that we meet from day to day. For with God nothing is
impossible, provided it falls within his will.

We believe that the Lord knows what is best for our
friends and neighbours. We will not therefore torment
ourselves with questions of what is appropriate for the

glory of God but, rather, expect great things from God. Some, for fear of raising false expectations, raise no expectations at all. Although we believe in a God of miracles, we are fearful lest people believe only because of the miracles. But Jesus himself encouraged his disciples to believe that he was truly God by believing his miracles if they could not believe his words. The truth is that from time to time the Lord works miracles for his own glory and purposes. As with the apostles, sometimes he chooses to confirm the authority of his messengers by a miraculous sign. His purposes are never in one direction. In showing his love and mercy, he wants to create love, faith and hope among his people.

Part of our difficulty is that we compartmentalize the workings of God. Things we cannot understand or explain fully we talk of as being supernatural, forgetting that God is also the Lord of the natural. His miraculous touch may be seen in the timing of events or the faithful supply of people or funds to sustain his work. The consistent way in which God cares and provides for his people is every bit as miraculous as the more spectacular signs of his presence.

The point is that as we pray we should count on God's love and generosity much more than we do. As a general rule God gives us much more than we deserve for he is generous. If then our expectation of him is high we will respond more readily to the promptings of his Holy Spirit. We will not hold back in unbelief. We will also raise the expectation of others. At the end of the day it is—as Jesus said—'According to your faith.'

This does not mean there are no mysteries and puzzles or, indeed, perplexing times. When God fails to send his help then we do well to remember the story of Lazarus and how Mary and Martha never doubted that Jesus was able to heal their brother and save him from dying. What they could not understand was the reason why he delayed his coming. In fact he had something more wonderful in store. When faced with perplexing situations we do well to believe that God has something better for us.

This came home to me with freshness recently when two sisters I know lost their brother. He died very suddenly in middle life and it was a hard thing for them to bear. At the post mortem it was discovered that he had a congenital heart condition that might well have left him a cripple in later years. Instead, God in his love took him home to heaven. The sisters had not doubted the love of God for their brother, but were reassured when they discovered the circumstances of his death.

When you talk like this there are always voices raised about the place of suffering in the Christian life. It is pointed out that some of the deepest experiences of God's love occur during times of suffering. Those are the secrets of the darkness. I am not advocating that we use prayer as an escape route from suffering, but it is certainly not Christian to succumb to blind resignation to circumstances, or adopt a fatalistic attitude to life. The Lord encourages us to pray our way through circumstances to a peaceful acceptance of his will, especially if he has chosen the way of suffering for our blessing. In the process we are often surprised at the way he transforms our situations. There are many more love gifts he wants us to enjoy than we suspect. Prayer is the way we discover how much God loves us.

There is of course a spirit we must avoid—that of unbelief. If we cry to God for some special love gift because we are questioning his love or his ability to provide, we are putting God to the test in a wrong way. Signs and wonders are not on demand to remove the need to trust God at all times. They are tokens of God's love for those who love him and do not question that love. If God withholds his love gifts his purpose may be to test our love for him and mature our trust in him. We may not realize it, but our requests may be very selfish and far from desiring the glory of God. The spirit of faith can expect great things of God, but is not stumbled if God's way is to withhold such things.

Prayer

Lord, you give us more than we ask or deserve in your great love. Help us to count on your generosity and not to limit your grace and mercy by our prayers. When there are mysteries keep us steadfast in our faith in you, and may we resist the temptation to question your love. We ask this through the One who laid down his life for his friends, Jesus Christ our Lord. Amen.

27

The Transforming Power of Prayer

Jesus taught us to love one another. Was that simply a
love for fellow Christians? If we only love fellow believers we are no better than unbelievers who do the
same for their friends. Jesus reached out to all alike,
friend and foe. This was the remarkable thing about him
and was in such contradistinction to the religious leaders
of his day. They were somewhat scandalized when he sat
down for a meal with tax collectors and 'sinners'. He was
even prepared to befriend a known adulteress. Jesus'
love knew no boundaries.

There is of course a special love between Christian
people which is clearly recognized by those who are not
believers. Believers, generally speaking, strike up a
quick friendship when they find common ground through
their faith in Jesus Christ. There is the family likeness,
the sharing of the one Spirit, by those who are born
again of the Spirit of God. Christian love is also practical. The New Testament word for love, *agape*, implies
glad sacrifice for another. Jesus is our model and we
follow him. There should be a willingness to lay down
our lives for one another and in that spirit serve in practical ways. This we find easy enough for those whom we

count our friends, but what about those we find difficult and to whom we are not attracted?

Jesus, by commanding us to love one another, is not implying that we will necessarily like everyone. It is possible to serve someone we do not particularly like. Liking people has a lot to do with personalities. But even if they clash, we can experience the transforming power of prayer. It is so often the case that we don't like certain people because either we don't really know them or we see them in the wrong light. If, however, we start praying for them it is wonderful how attitudes can change. The biggest change is usually in ourselves. If we pray for someone then we're not far off loving him. As the Spirit of God enters our hearts and leads us in intercession for that person, God pours love into our hearts and drives out dislike.

The greatest victory of the Christian life is love for one's enemies. Jesus taught us that we are to love our enemies and do good to them. Such love does not come naturally, but it can be received through prayer. For it is through prayer that we put on the very likeness of Christ and draw on his love. It is possible to say as Jesus did, 'Father forgive them, for they know not what they do.' If we find hate, anger and bitterness crowding into our hearts we need to drive such things out by prayer. If we cannot pray for ourselves in this matter, it is helpful to ask others to pray for us. The importance of winning through in this area is too great to spurn such help. Many have experienced the power of love for their enemies and have seen the victory that comes through prayer.

Jesus' teaching on love commands us to confess our sins to one another. He taught that if in 'bringing a gift to the altar' we remember that someone has something against us, we are to go to him and be reconciled before we worship the Lord. We find this very difficult. We have to pray for God's grace to do it. Similarly, if we have been hurt, we need to forgive those who have hurt us if our prayers are not to be hindered. In many cases we are hurt because we are bearing the wounds of Christ. Suffering is a part of our Christian life. As Jesus said, 'If the world hates you, know that it has hated me before it hated you' (John 15:18). When the hurt comes from fellow believers, because we forget that they too are sinners, we find it even more difficult to forgive. We do not expect to be hurt by fellow members of the body of Christ, and it is in such situations that we need to learn the transforming power of prayer. How many divided churches could be healed if there was more attention to Jesus' teaching and the discovery of the effectiveness of prayer in helping us to do what we know is right when relationships have been damaged. We all need God's grace to admit that we have not only been wrong, but have also fallen into sin. The joy of Jesus' teaching is that when we have repented in this way the matter of forgiving others becomes easier.

The East African revivals majored on this theme of confession, repentance and restoration. The Holy Spirit created a beautiful spirit of humility and love among Christians. There were extremes, as there often are when revival comes, but the willingness on behalf of Christians to admit openly their sin led to reconciliation and the transformation of the church. Some became oversensitive and needed to be reminded that we confess sin to the one we have offended, but only to the church if the wider community has been hurt. If relationships are not as they should be in my life, at home, at work or in my church, then there is something more I have to discover about the transforming power of prayer.

Prayer

We thank you, Lord, that when you were reviled and mocked, you did not retaliate but loved your enemies. Give us grace to love those we find it hard to like, and to pray for those who oppose us because we belong to you. May we walk in the steps of the Saviour and receive his life-transforming power, to the honour of his name and the extension of his kingdom. Amen.

28

Fleeing From His Presence

The prophet Jonah tried to run away from God. He discovered that he could not. God put him through a very turbulent time until he came to his senses. He saw in all his troubles the hand of God, and so was able to say, 'All thy waves and thy billows have passed over me' (Jonah 2:3). He then got up and went and did what God had asked him to do in the first place.

Many people run away from the will of God for their lives. Although they say they believe in a God of love, in practice they deny it. God's will for our life can only be the best. People run away for many reasons. There is the fear of not being able to cope or that they will miss out on something good. Some do not like the thought of being mocked for their choice of career.

In many more cases, however, it is that expectations have not been met, or there have been disappointments. People come to the end of the road. They feel that they are through with knowing and loving God. He hasn't worked things out the way they hoped. They feel let down, and that somehow God hasn't been fair. But sometimes such people fail to ask basic questions. Have they been keeping God's laws? Have their priorities

been right? Have they been sensitive to their own conscience? And, above all, have they been living in God's
presence through daily prayer? When such questions are
asked, often you find there has been a steady spiritual
decline over many years.

The decline started when prayer was abandoned and
God no longer got a look in. Having reaped what was
sown, people over-react and decide to walk out on God.
But God in his mercy continues to pursue us. There is
always the possibility of turning back to him. We may
have started our Christian lives by welcoming Jesus into
our house, but failed to allow him to order and arrange
the rooms as he sees best. He needs a fresh invitation to
take charge and sort out our lives. If, however, we continued to shut God out of our lives there is only the awful
prospect of judgement. Jesus himself warned that a day
would come for many when he would have to say, 'I
never knew you; depart from me' (Matthew 7:23). To be
shut out of God's presence in life is bad enough. For
eternity it is beyond imagination. It is however a real
possibility.

What can we do for those who are running away from
God? How many parents there are who agonize over
children who start well but then turn away from following the Lord. This is the inside unseen story of many
Christian homes, especially those of full-time Christian
ministers and workers. Rather than try to drag such
children back into the kingdom of God we must rely
upon the power of prayer. God has his own ways of
bringing people to their senses. It may appear that he is
heedless of our prayers for many years and yet he is at
work. There needs to be unending trust and patience.
We need an inexhaustible capacity to believe that God is
in charge of the situation. There is many a story of the
children of Christian ministers and workers fleeing from

the presence of God, only to find him in their dire need. God has his servants all over the world and those for whom we pray are within his grasp. Some of us need to let go of our children a little more and allow God to get hold of them. When we see our friends fleeing from the presence of God we need to pray that they will run into the arms of the Saviour.

A talented young teenager dropped out of school, to the despair of his parents, and worked nights as an entertainer in Malaysia. One night he decided to throw in an old Christian song he knew from earlier days. That very night another young man from a local Pentecostal church had been guided by God to the night club. A friendship between the two was struck, and without realizing it this talented musician had run once again into the presence of God. How many similar true stories might be told.

Instead of faith inspiring prayer, we resort to cajoling and persuasion. In some cases parents are more concerned about their own reputation and standing in Christian circles. Rather than loving those who are running away, we adopt a judgemental attitude and fail to show compassion when things go wrong. It may be that God is chastening his child, but it is better for the back-slider to draw that conclusion than for us to assume too quickly that is the correct interpretation of events. The prodigal in Jesus' parable 'came to himself' by himself. God is well able to answer our prayers for others to do the same. Our confidence is that no one can escape his presence for even if I 'dwell in the uttermost parts of the sea', God is there (Psalm 139:9). That is comforting to a Christian and should also be a reminder that God in his own time and in his own way is able to get closer to modern day Jonahs than anyone else.

Prayer

Thank you, Lord, that we cannot run away from you. Even if we go to the other end of the world you are there. We pray for any who have turned their backs on you and are running away from your love. In your loving and yet firm way turn them back to you, for you are the Way, the Truth and the Life and no one comes to the Father but by you. We have no other resting place except your Father's house. We ask this in your name. Amen.

29

Entering Heaven

Paul describes death as the last great enemy. Death cannot be mocked. But it can be overcome. Jesus has overcome death through his resurrection, which in turn is the
guarantee of our own. Faith in the resurrection and an
experience of the living, risen Lord Jesus takes away the
fear of death. Death is not natural to the body. It is not
what God originally planned, but is in fact God's curse
for sin. Christ died on the cross to bear that curse and
remove the fear of condemnation for sin, which Paul
describes as the 'sting of death'. For not only do we
shrink from death, but also from a day of reckoning we
know we cannot face. The gospel meets both fears and
teaches us how to be reconciled to God and enjoy peace
with him. This gives us peace about the issue of death.
We can live free of its fear.

There is, however, a natural fear about dying. This
fear can be overcome, even by unbelievers. Hardly a
year goes by without some award for gallantry. There
are heroic attempts to save life at sea, in the mountains
or down the potholes. The bravery of soldiers in battle is
recognized. Once again the Victoria Cross was awarded
in recognition of particular bravery in the battle to take

the Falkland Islands. In an emergency a higher ideal drives back our fears and gives special courage. The Christian has more grounds for courage and the highest motivation. As Jesus both taught and demonstrated, 'Greater love has no man than this, that a man lay down his life for his friends' (John 15:13).

Nevertheless many, Christians included, are afraid of dying. It is not so much death that is feared but the dying process. If we could simply transfer from one body to another—which is what is promised to us when Christ returns—we would not be fearful. Christians look forward to the return of the Lord Jesus because he will change our present body, which humbles us so much, to become like his own glorious resurrection body. As Paul put it, 'We shall not all sleep, but we shall all be changed' (1 Corinthians 15:51). Paul prefers to call death a sleep. None of us is afraid to go to sleep. (That is unless we suspect that we might not wake up again, which is surely part of the fear some face who have to undergo surgery.) The Christian message is that we will wake up, whatever happens, if not on earth, then in heaven. But many of us would prefer not to have to experience the sleep of death. We shrink from the dying process.

Old people, of course, do have a different perspective on this. Sometimes they are so tired they just long to fall asleep and go to heaven. They have grown weary with life and would much rather transfer to the next world. But even old peole have their fears, as their body gradually gives way into death. We need to remember that wise saying of Robert Murray McCheyne. He said that many people, Christians included, are afraid to die. 'But what they forget,' he said, 'is that God gives dying grace to the dying and not to the living.' In other words, God's grace is always sufficient for the hour of need. Since prayer is one of the major means of grace, we need to learn to pray with our loved ones as they pass from this life to the next.

I remember speaking once to the Matron of the CIM retired workers' home in Pembury, Kent. She had nursed many of the missionaries on their deathbed and seen them cross over to heaven. When I said this must be rather a harrowing experience for her, she smiled at me as if I had a lot to learn about the Christian life. She did agree, however, that many do become frightened. She went on to explain that at such times prayer can bring peace and take away fear. By helping the dying through prayer to focus on the risen Lord, the vision of heaven begins to burn brightly and fear subsides. She believed that many literally had some kind of vision of the Lord before dying, which was a great help to them.

Clearly it is possible to be totally in control of the human frame as death approaches. Jesus was totally in charge as he hung on the cross, as he had been throughout his life. In a very deliberate act he commended his spirit to God, his Father, and died. The gospels point out that he died sooner than expected, making the breaking of the legs unnecessary. Even in death God was wonderfully merciful to his own Son. And so he is to his children, giving them special grace and peace to cope with the unknown. Once believers have gone home to heaven we can only rejoice. As Paul put it, 'Away from the body and at home with the Lord' (2 Corinthians 5:8). They have gone to be with Christ which is far better. It is better because they are delivered from 'the burden of the flesh' as the old Book of Common Prayer puts it, and are enjoying the full liberty of the children of God. They are in the glory and if the curtain of eternity were to be drawn back we would see them in their glorious new bodies. There was a glimpse of that when Jesus was transfigured on the mountain, for there appeared with him Moses and Elijah. These two men one assumes were in their glorified bodies, for they were recognized by Peter. The apostle wanted to stay with them, but there was still important work to be done. Jesus and his disciples had to come down from the mountain top and face the reality of gaining the victory over sin and death through the cross.

If we understand heaven properly then once people have died there is no longer any point in praying for them. There is nothing that we can ask that they should enjoy, for they are in perfect happiness. And if they have not gone to heaven but rather to hell, then it is too late for change. Prayers for the dead are therefore both unhelpful and misleading. Those who pray for the dead usually lack Christian teaching and therefore Christian assurance. There is nothing in the Bible which suggests that purgatory is a reality or necessary. It teaches the reverse, assuring the believer of a full atonement for sins committed through the death of Christ. The Bible says quite simply that when we see him we shall be like him. The entrance to heaven brings not only final victory over death but also sin. At long last after a life-long struggle to be holy, we live up to our name of saints. What a wonderful place heaven must be, where those things that spoil our relationships here on earth are finally taken away and we can enjoy unbroken communion with God and one another.

Another craving of unbelievers to be avoided is the desire to make contact with the dead through mediums. This is firmly forbidden in the Bible and there seem to be good reasons for it. For one thing, it is an unkindness to bring people back from heaven to this world. Jean Darnall in her book *Heaven Here I Come* recalls how, following her mother's death, she cried to God immediately that he would bring her back. The Lord graciously permitted her mother to return to life. Jean was greeted with the question of why she had called her back from heaven, for it was so much better there. So even that understandable prayer was inappropriate. Mediums, of course, are in touch with the world of demons. The devil is the arch deceiver and any communication that comes through a medium is nothing but pure deception. That is not to say it is without reality. Contact with mediums only serves to bring people more under the power of the devil and his evil angels. At the end of the day, an attempt to contact the dead expresses man's utter selfishness, because people are not really sorry for the deceased, but for themselves. People are full of self-pity because they have lost a companion. It is during bereavement that we especially need the companionship of the Lord Jesus and his Spirit to reassure us of his love and future provision for us in heaven.

Prayer

O Lord, you have made us and you know that we are but dust. When we are weak and dying, support us by your love and take away our fears. Reassure us, risen Lord, of your power to raise us from the grave that we may die in hope of that last great day, when you will change our frail bodies to be like your glorious risen body. All powers will be restored and all our friendships renewed in your glorious and everlasting kingdom. To you be all the praise and all the glory. Amen.

30

Robbing God

This book has been written because of a concern over the dwindling prayer life of the church. The fact that we feel we can do without prayer says something about our human pride and self-confidence. We may be Christian people, but we cannot live without Christ's help. We may be called to be Christian workers, but we cannot succeed without being workers together with Christ. Without prayer, therefore, our Christian life is likely to be without the fruits of righteousness and our Christian service ineffective. But there is another way of looking at all this.

The gospel writers considered the cleansing of the temple by the Lord Jesus to be highly significant. Jesus was seldom angry during his earthly life, but when he entered the temple and discovered that it was no longer a house of prayer, righteous indignation rose to the surface. He drove out the money-changers and those who were selling. This was high drama. There was more to it than driving out those cashing in on religion. He had come to overturn the wrong use of the temple and bring in the right. The temple or the house of God is above all a place for prayer.

I used to think that the main thrust of his saying that those buying and selling in the temple had created a den of robbers, referred to the high rate of money exchange, and the high price of merchandise. No doubt that *was* involved, but Jesus went beyond that to see the implications of the absence of prayer in the temple. It was that God was being robbed of the opportunity for fellowship with his people, of speaking to them and guiding them in their responsibility to reach out to all nations with the good news. In that sense those in the temple were robbing God of the opportunity to glorify his name among the nations.

By our neglect of prayer, are we robbing God? If we fail to pray how can we receive his guidance? If there is little prayer is it not to be expected that there are few who are called out to preach the gospel among the nations? If prayer is neglected God is robbed of the opportunity to change our lives so that they speak to others. We rob God of all the potential of which we have been speaking. This is a great robbery. We would not dream of robbing God.

But this isn't the only subject over which the Lord had to challenge God's people concerning robbery. There was the matter of their tithes and offerings and the way sometimes we hold back what is due to God. Not that releasing a tenth of our income fulfils all that God requires, but it does express clearly our understanding that all our money belongs to God and is under his control. It is to be released and used as he wants. Christians have found that once they have settled the matter of the tithe, they receive a greater spirit of generosity and give beyond their imagination. They are surprised by their new capacity for generosity. In this way God releases us from materialism. Likewise with prayer. If we would but tithe our time for prayer we would soon find that a fresh delight in prayer comes into our lives. Prayer will become what it should be: not a duty but a lifestyle. We will quickly learn to bring everything to God in prayer. Above all we will be very anxious not to rob him of the potential for glorifying his name in and through us, out into the world. We will discover the hidden resources that are received through prayer. God's power will be unlocked to do the things he alone can do.

Does the Lord need to come to the temple of God's people again today to cleanse us afresh? For we are the living stones of God's temple. Do we need to be forgiven for our neglect of one of God's most precious gifts? Do we need to repent of the sins of pride, independence and self-confidence? If there is to be revival in our land the Lord must visit and cleanse the temple afresh. And as has been well said, revival in the church begins with revival in my life. It is time to invite the Lord by his Spirit to come and restore to us a life of prayer.

Prayer

Almighty God, forgive our neglect of prayer, and if we have unwittingly robbed you of your rightful place in our lives, we ask your forgiveness. If we have made your temple a den of robbers, by not listening to you in prayer, so limiting your power among us, cleanse us afresh and renew us by your Spirit that we may once again be a holy priesthood, interceding for the coming of your kingdom, through Jesus Christ our Lord. Amen.

Epilogue

It is one thing to read a book about prayer. It is quite
another to pray! The best advice that I can give concerning how to pray is to invite you to pray the prayer at the
end of each chapter. The prayers have been written in
the plural because we need to pray together and regain a
lost art and a missing gap in the life of many a local
church. We learn as we pray. We learn a great deal also
from others as we listen to their prayers. It can also help
to use the prayers that godly men down the ages have
written. There is great value in liturgical prayers which
have stood the test of time and can expand the breadth
of our praying.

Our faith will grow, if we take the trouble to record
prayer requests and put a tick in the answer column
when God meets our requests. Those who have been
disciplined enough to do this can turn back over the
pages of their prayer diary recording God's faithfulness
in answering prayer. Those who pray regularly have
fewer problems concerning prayer than those who only
pray when faced with an emergency. Prayer above all
should become a way of life. Like the Lord Jesus we
should seek unbroken communion with God our Father.

EPILOGUE

At the end of the day that is what prayer is all about—a relationship with God.

Bibliography

J. Oswald Sanders, *Prayer Power Unlimited* (Highland Books, 1985).

Samuel Chadwick, *The Path of Prayer* (Hodder & Stoughton, 1963).

J. Oswald Sanders, *Effective Prayer* (OMF Books, 1961).

E. M. Bounds, *Power through Prayer* (Marshalls, 1931).

Merlin R. Carothers, *Power in Praise* (Kingsway Publications, 1974).

Arthur Wallis, *Pray in the Spirit* (Kingsway Publications, 1970).

R. A. Torrey, *How to Pray* (Lakeland Series, Oliphant, 1903).

John White, *People in Prayer* (IVP, 1978).

D. L. Moody, *Prevailing Prayer* (Marshalls, n.d.).

E. M. Blaiklock, *Our Lord's Teaching on Prayer* (Oliphant, n.d.).

R. Arthur Mathews, *Born for Battle* (OMF Books/STL, 1982).

David Watson, *Hidden Warfare* (STL/Kingsway Publications, 1987).

Leonard Ravenhill, *Why Revival Tarries* (STL Books, 1972).

P. T. Forsyth, *The Soul of Prayer* (Independent Press London, 1916).

Eileen Crossman, *Mountain Rain* (OMF Books, 1984).

The Father Heart of God

by Floyd McClung

What is God like?

Has he got time for twentieth-century men and women?

Does he really care?

In his work with *Youth with a Mission*, Floyd McClung has met many who suffer from deep emotional hurts and fears.

Time and again it has been the discovery of God as Father—perfect and reliable, unlike any human parent—that has brought healing and liberty.

This book is for you...

...if you find it hard to accept God as a loving father, or
...if you know God's love but would like to share his blessing with others more effectively.

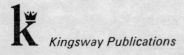

Kingsway Publications

Standing In The Gap

by Ken Gardiner

'God bless Africa, and Mummy and Daddy too. Amen.'

A childish prayer—yet so often our own prayer life has advanced little beyond the vague wish that God will bless somebody somewhere. If we do become more specific, we are often quick to present God with our own desires and ask for little more than his seal of approval—'if it is your will'.

Yet many Christians really want to know God's will and pray with confidence and authority.

With this in mind, Ken Gardiner reminds us of our position in Christ. Carefully and convincingly he applies biblical truths to the practice of prayer, showing how we can stand in the gap between heaven's supply and the world's need.

Ken Gardiner is Vicar of St Philip & St James, Chatham. He has taught on prayer for both radio and inter-church gatherings.

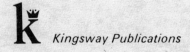

Kingsway Publications

Praying Together

by Mike & Katey Morris

We can all pray on our own. We can know the power of praying with other Christians too.

But what about praying with our marriage partner? Why is it such a problem? Can prayer be fun? Can we worship at home?

If you have ever asked one of these questions, and if you long for greater spiritual unity with your husband or wife, then this book is for you.

This is not a lecture on 'why you should pray more', but a personal and practical manual that will spur you on to action, so that prayer with your partner becomes a living reality, not just some hopeless ideal.

Mike Morris is the Research and Development Officer at the Evangelical Alliance and **Katey** is a secondary school teacher. The seminars that they have led at various Bible-week conventions have shown the enormous need for their practical and spiritual teaching.

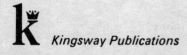

Kingsway Publications